My Recovery Walk with Jesus

From Bondage to Freedom

By

Dawn Louise Williams

1

Dedicated to my husband
Rick Williams:
For always thinking I'm the crowned jewel
in your life and for listening as I read aloud
each and every devotional.

I truly could not have written this book without you.

Table of Contents

7

Forewords:

Addiction is born out of the common, fallen state of man. If we're honest, we must admit we are all addicted to something — some are apparent, some are illegal, but all are enslaving. This book is about the movement from slavery to freedom through honesty and grace. Born out of an honest encounter with the grace of God in the death and resurrection of Jesus Christ, Dawn Williams' book offers real hope and real help. Dawn's book follows the proven Twelve Steps in its organization, but it's true power flows from God's Word which suffuses these pages. Combining carefully chosen statements of truth with raw honesty and experienced insight, this book is a pathway for our recovery walk with Jesus. It is the effective medicine of wise counsel in the daily dose we need.

Pastor Greg Williams
Former Associate Pastor, Christ Community Church, Ashburn Va..
Retired Deputy Associate Administrator for Human Exploration and Operations, National Aeronautics Space Administration

One of the challenges facing the Christian Church is to take Bill Wilson's successful *Alcoholics Anonymous* "Twelve-Step" program and make it compatible with Christian truth. Wilson identifies God as a mere "higher power" or "God as you understand him." This is out of step with the God of Scripture who has revealed himself in the person of Jesus Christ as the Triune God, not simply a "higher power." Dawn Williams, a recovering alcoholic, has embraced that challenge and skillfully presents thirty, Christ-centered, Bible-based devotions for each of the first four, foundational steps of the Twelve-Step program. Cutting through the typical excuses of those addicted to drugs, alcohol, and pornography, Williams presents the only solution: a relationship with God through Jesus Christ.

This is a vital resource for churches and Christian recovery groups ministering to those suffering from addiction. Copies should be readily available on the shelves of every church library and Pastor's study.

Pastor Don Matzat
Pastor, Lutheran Church-Missouri Synod
Author: *Christ-Esteem, Truly-Transformed* and *Inner Healing: Deliverance or Deception?*

In, "My Recovery Walk With Jesus," Dawn does not offer encouragement to us from the perspective of someone who has never walked the complicated roads of recovery. Instead, she speaks front-row encouragement and insights into the beautiful and powerful walk of recovery with Jesus. This is, hands down, the most powerful recovery devotional I have ever seen. You're going to love it!

Pastor Jim Ladd
Senior Pastor, Evergreen Christian Community Church, Olympia Washington
Author: *The Pursuit: 40 Days/40 Biblical Truths*

10

Preface:

"The Spirit of the Lord is on me, because he has anointed me to preach good news to the poor. He has sent me to proclaim freedom for the prisoners and recovery of sight for the blind, to release the oppressed, to proclaim the year of the Lord's favor." Luke 4: 18-19

It was January of 1987 and I had no idea life as I knew it was about to change forever! I was a mess and felt hopeless beyond repair. I couldn't be the daughter my parents wanted or the mother my child deserved. As I left my ex-husband's house my emotions tumbled inside my head as tears made their way down my face.

Unable to raise my daughter anymore due to my substance use, I had agreed to sign over custody. There was no provision for visitation, but many promises of "you can see her when you want." I knew this wasn't true and that I might never see my daughter again. I felt smashed, destroyed and filled with desperation and truly didn't want to live anymore. Suicidal thoughts were an ever present companion. I was fractured into a million pieces and nothing I did could fix me.

As I drove away down the highway I cried out to God, "Help me God! What do I do? I can't just let my little girl go!" I stared up at the broad expanse of the highway bridge and my chest was so tight from pain it felt like my heart was going to explode.

All of the sudden, I heard a voice. It wasn't loud, angry or even audible but was gentle, sweet, and compassionate. The voice said, "Go to treatment." In that moment, my life changed forever! On January 12, 1987, I entered into treatment for alcohol and drug addiction and learned that I had a condition that was killing me physically, emotionally and spiritually. I learned what addiction was, realized that I had it, and found out what I needed to do to manage my recovery from it. The miraculous had happened and my heart soared with hope.

I was told to go to Twelve-Step meetings every day, get a sponsor, work the steps and don't use alcohol or drugs in-between. It was tough changing my whole life, but I had Jesus in my pocket and felt intense gratitude for the way He scooped me up and set my feet on the path of recovery.

I was a hair-stylist by trade and knew I wouldn't be able to support my little family on a minimum wage job. So, I started back to school and selected psychology as my major of study. My recovery was secure and stable, yet rebellion was percolating with my new experiences of success. I knew that God had rescued me from addiction but that didn't prevent me from blaming Him for all of my failures, the failures of others and what I thought was a really awful childhood.

I began to study the different paradigms of psychology, metaphysical aspects of the spiritual realm of enlightenment, and my faith in God started to waiver. Christianity taught me that I was born into sin and needed a savior, but psychology taught me that I was born *tabula-rasa* (with a blank slate) and it was poor parenting, unfair work wages for women, a male god, and awful men who created my addiction! Surely, if I could travel the enlightened path I would enter a state of Nirvana. Didn't need God for that!

As my faith waivered, my resentments against Christianity festered and grew. I began to storm out of Twelve-Step meetings when anyone mentioned the Christian God. But God, being the loving and faithful Father, would stay close to me despite my rebellion. He would reveal Himself to me well into my 7th year

12

of recovery as the loving, committed and no-nonsense God that He is!

During this time of my recovery, so many changes were happening. I had ended a long term relationship, found out that my therapist of many years (including my thirty-day treatment stay) had relapsed, received my Master's Degree in clinical psychology and addiction studies. I began attending a Unitarian church. However, the biggest change that happened was my discovery that church isn't church without the Spirit of Christ!

God used each and every situation in my life to proclaim His awesome healing power and continue to help me see Him. In 1995, I met the love of my life, Rick (AKA KL Williams the most awesome blues guitarist I've ever known!). It was a beautiful experience to truly fall in love and receive love in a way I never thought possible. I had already started to warm back up to the idea of Jesus in my life, and the greatest shared interest Rick and I had was growing deeper in a relationship with God.

For the first time in many years, hearing the name of Jesus didn't fill me with rage. I had stopped attending the Unitarian Church and started dabbling in different Christian churches that my recovery friends talked about. All of the sudden, I didn't feel resentment, short-changed or full of shame.

God is so good! Rick asked me to marry him, and for someone who vowed never to be married or have children again, I quickly said yes. Everything changed. We had so much in common and the most important shared hope was experiencing a new and tender belief in Jesus. One of our friends was attending a Lutheran church in Marysville, WA and we were looking for a church for our wedding. So, we started to attend services (my motives were to join the church, so we didn't have to pay a rental fee!)

It's funny how God works because there was no charge to use the church for our wedding! We started pre-marital counseling with the pastor, got married and settled into life as a married couple. You would think God had done enough, but He was just getting started!

"My Recovery Walk with Jesus" is a devotional that is born from the pain and joy of my own recovery from alcoholism and drug addiction and my journey back to Jesus. If God can take a life like mine, restore my sight and prepare me to minister to others, He can and will do the same for you! I am presently employed by the Washington State Department of Corrections as the Administrator for the prison drug and alcohol programs.

May God bless you and keep you and make His face shine upon you!

Dawn Louise Williams
Olympia, Washington, 2019

Step One

"We admitted we were powerless over alcohol
– that our lives had become unmanageable."
Alcoholics Anonymous

Day 1: *Finding Comfort in Defeat*

> *"You, God, are my God, earnestly I seek you;*
> *I thirst for you, my whole being longs for you, in a dry and weary*
> *land where there is no water. . . .. Because you are my help,*
> *I sing in the shadow of your wings." Psalm 63:1, 7.*

It seems like a lifetime has gone by since we walked through the doors of treatment or found ourselves seated with people just like us in the rooms of a Twelve-Step program. There are lots of different ways we show up; maybe it's our first attempt at recovery, or we're fresh from a relapse. But one thing we have in common—and there are many—is that our addiction has left bruises from the top of our heads to the tips of our toes and everywhere in between!

It's strange though that we find comfort sitting in a room with people seeking relief from this sense of loneliness, longing and unquestionable defeat. Little by little, God is showing us how to resist the drugs, food, alcohol, gambling, pornography, and destructive relationships that twist and contort the vision God has for our lives. He is giving us the eyes to see and the ears to hear as it dawns on us that those friends weren't really friends after all.

The relationships we thought loving really only brought destructive pain and did nothing to soothe our sense of loneliness and longing. Early recovery overwhelms us with feelings of despair. And for the first time in many years, we find ourselves crying out to God for help. Despair drives away doubt and we believe God is the only power who can relieve us from the pain, confusion, and demoralization we suffered in our addiction. David's prayer, now ours, is the beginning of our lifelong commitment to recovery.

When our power ends, God's power begins. He folds us under the shadow of His wings, and we feel safe, secure, and relieved. Earnest in our desire for change, we leave behind the substances, people, places, and things that blocked us from God. Our thirst for change is one only God can quench, and we welcome His presence into our lives every moment of every day. We are beginning to trust that God has come to set this captive free.

Lord, today – tucked safely under the shadow of Your wing – keep me clean and sober, focused on You for I know that without You there is no hope. My thoughts are jumbled and confused so I need You to speak to my heart! Help me live out my day in Your presence.

Day 2: *On the Cross of Hope*

"That is why I say to run from sex sin. No other sin affects the body
as this one does. When you sin this sin, it is against your own
body. Haven't you yet learned that your body is the home of the Holy
Spirit God gave you, and that he lives within you? Your own body
does not belong to you. For God has bought you with a great price.
So, use every part of your body to give glory back to God because he
owns it." 1 Corinthians 6:18–20
(The Living Bible)[1]

Twirling like a cyclone as we sought pleasure, we have left in our wake pain, destruction, and chaos. Our incessant drives continued to lead us headlong into trouble. But after a while, nothing we used, ate, or did could bring us the feeling of our first high. We may have traveled from one club to another night after night. And though we may have found a Prince/Princess Charming here or there, it wasn't long before he/she turned into Mr. or Ms. Icky!

But today, we are no longer controlled by our unmet needs, wants, or desires and are coming to realize how we abused ourselves. There is hope in this recognition, because we understand that we don't have to do this anymore! Jesus redeemed us and called us by name. He went to the cross so that we could live and be set free! On that cross of hope, as He rose from the dead, so did we.

Despite our flaws and faithless, feeble hearts, God still invites us to bring all our troubles to Him. Until our last breath, He will give us hope as He lives in and around us. God is

---

[1] *The Living Bible*, (Tyndale House Publishers, 1974.)

19

revealing to us the hope and power of Jesus and is 100 percent for us! We open our hearts and admit that without Him our lives are full of unmanageability and chaos. Step One helps usher in recovery and creates a space in our hearts for God. We are full of gratitude, because we know that God has reached in and pulled us out from under the hopelessness of our addiction!

God, thank You for sending your Son who even now lives in my heart. Today, let me honor my body as Your temple, designed and predestined as Your own. I am Yours, and You are mine. Let me hear and feel You today in every thought and uttered word heard or spoken.

✟

Day 3: *Rehearsing the Mess*

"Isaiah was right when he prophesied about you hypocrites; as it is written: 'These people honor me with their lips, but their hearts are far from me. They worship me in vain; their teachings are but merely human rules taught by men.'" Mark 7:6–7.

In early recovery, we are truly desperate people! It is disappointing that the desperation does not end just because we're not using substances, gambling, pornography, and food or shopping till we drop! Some of us come into the Twelve-Step programs and learn how to *"talk the talk"* but haven't yet experienced what it means to *"walk the walk."* In meetings, we have an internal conversation with ourselves, thinking of all the things we'd say if called on!

This internal conversation might include whether we agree or disagree with what we have heard. Grandiose thinking turns us into spiritual giants in our own minds and we begin to judge people against the high opinions we have of ourselves. But then we get called on and not one rehearsed word come out of our mouths, and if it does, it seems to fall flat: no one laughs or coos about how awesome we are!

But God is good and love us anyway. He comes alongside us and whispers that He loves and cares for us, and He offers us a hand to climb down from our soapbox. Shame is an ever-present companion and tempts us to judge ourselves harshly. But God wants us to take His hand in childlike faith and listen to His gentle laughter of love.

He longs for us to turn to Him with our hurts, disappointments, and feelings of powerlessness. We are sick, desperate, and needy and our bodies may still be toxic with an obsessive never-ending loop of thoughts: But we are not hopeless! God has been gracious to us and is infusing into our hearts the desire to please Him. We long to learn more about God and how much He loves us! God is absolutely crazy about us!

Ever so slowly we are committing ourselves to recovery and learning how to walk in faith. In early recovery, confusion and the need for change are ever present, but we remind ourselves that our God is one of peace rather than confusion. We are not perfect and are still soul-sick in so many ways, but we trust that God will continue to heal us and keep us sober.

God, today let my life be truth and let any words that flow from my lips be honest and sincere. Help me hear You when lies tumble out, or when lies are manifested inwards. Lord of life let my life be an offering of worship to You.

Day 4: *Jesus be Mine*

"Have faith in God." Mark 11:22.

Mark 11:22 is such a short yet powerful (and easy to memorize) verse. In active addiction we had placed our faith and trust in so many different things: people, substances, beauty products, gimmicks that promised us fame and fortune, clothes, extravagant dwellings, or expensive fancy cars, and money — lots and lots of money.

As we work Step One, we acknowledge that when we place our hope and aspirations on the things of this world and focus on them, we always walk away disappointed. We have tried many different substances and many different substitutes — new relationships, old relationships, new cars, old cars, new jobs, and the list goes on — to change how we feel just to experience faith in something . . . anything.

Some of us have sought and achieved fame, yet we are seldom happy and eventually the shine wears off our star because there is always someone waiting in the wings to steal the spotlight. Money comes and goes, a new car fast becomes an old car, and a new big house becomes worn and lived in as the sheen wears off the new granite countertops.

Before sobriety we were driven by a never-ending stream of deluded thoughts. We did not realize, blinded as we were by our addiction, that we were being controlled by its drives and needs as it took on a life of its own. Addiction took over our minds and bodies as it struggled to survive and started to take everything from us giving us nothing in return.

Our addiction proceeded unabashedly to make us believe with an unwavering faith that this drug, relationship, or material possession would relieve us of our sadness, depression, or loneliness and give us the joy and happiness we desired. But the little voice inside beckoned us to break free from the chains wrapped so heavily around our necks confining us to the never-ending cycle of despair. We admitted that we could not break free from these chains with our own power. While addiction had seemingly defeated us, in mercy, God reached out, grabbed onto us, and rescued us from certain death.

God, today I do have faith in You. I believe you love me and sent Jesus to save me. Help me, God, for I cling to Your promise of salvation. Jesus be mine. Live in me; show me more of who You are and who I really am in You.

Day 5: *Knowing You Jesus*

"What is impossible with man is possible with God." Luke 18:27.

There are so many well-meaning people that worked diligently to help us become sober and obtain housing, food or clothing. Some of us turned to panhandling and set up shop on a street corner holding a sign "need money" or "will work for food" or a highly successful sign that says, "Honestly I just need beer."

With altruistic motives, the people who reach out and try to help us hope we will respond to the kindness they offer. In their heart of hearts, they believe they can help change our lives by giving to us freely from their wallets or bringing us food or gifts during the Christmas holiday. There are so many wonderful people in our communities who truly want to help us.

But we use these people, whether they are professionals or family members, because the beast (addiction) living inside of us must be fed. Our addictions are bottomless in their appetites. Countless are the people who have tried to help, whether it was a professional who counseled us and gave us a grand strategy to stay clean and sober, or a family member who practiced tough love and told us to go get clean because they were not willing to have us around until we changed.

Perhaps for a time these people and their strategies were helpful and successful as our addiction was temporarily arrested and recovery began to emerge. But relapse was ever at our heels until we were completely convinced that substances were no longer the answer.

Having tried countless ways to rid ourselves of addiction like drinking only on the weekends or special holidays, only

25

using this drug instead of the other, ordering a salad from the fast-food restaurant, or just going to the casino for the buffet, it became obvious to us that we believed our own delusions.

We have become convinced that man, including ourselves, does not have the power to relieve us of our addiction, because we have repeated experiences with these failed attempts. As we look to the heavens, we finally arrive at a place where there is real hope when we admit that only God can relieve us of our addiction.

Today, emboldened by the force and power of God we realize that healing is possible because He loves us and longs for us to turn from the bondage that has held us captive and place our hope in Him. What a wonderful and beautiful recognition and promise of hope!

God, all the times I failed, and all the times man's efforts to change me have failed has shown me how much I need You. Your love never fails, and I believe that all things are possible for those who love You. Help me see You, God. I want You and need You. My life depends upon knowing You.

Day 6: *The Secret Club*

"This is how much God loved the world: He gave his Son, his one and only Son. And this is why: so that no one need be destroyed; by believing in him, anyone can have a whole and lasting life. God didn't go to all the trouble of sending his Son merely to point an accusing finger, telling the world how bad it was. He came to help, to put the world right again. Anyone who trusts in him is acquitted; anyone who refuses to trust him has long since been under the death sentence without knowing it. And why? Because of that person's failure to believe in the one-of-a-kind Son of God when introduced to him."
John 3:16–18.
(The Message)[2]

Such awe-inspiring verses of love and promise! Many of us thought that because we uttered the prayer of salvation we got our own get-out-of-jail-free card. We threw caution to the wind and were reckless, using substances until we were nearly unconscious, broke, hundreds of pounds overweight, or betrayed and abandoned by our families.

Addiction tried to rob us of the most rewarding relationship we will ever know and throw us into the abyss of shameful and decadent living. Vividly, we remember how people in bars, taverns and clubs, both young and old, with drink in hand stumbled from one new acquaintance to the other, attesting to be a member of this secret club called "Christian." The heart-felt experience of this verse was nonexistent in our lives, and our response to Jesus being nailed to the cross was lackluster at best. We seemed clueless and unresponsive to the sacrifice God made for His creation.

---

[2] Eugene H. Peterson, *The Message*, (NavPress, 2016)

The truth didn't sink in that instead of giving us over to the death we deserved, He gave us eternal life! We are sinners who had the soul-sick nerve to throw His name about in bars, taverns, dope houses, liquor stores, and pot shops as if He were a leftover piece of dung on our shoe.

It isn't until we're beaten, rejected and despised for and because of our addiction that we are able to understand the feelings Jesus may have had. While we are chin-deep in sin, Christ was perfect and sinless, yet He was rejected and crucified so we might have the awesome gift of being able to call on God and be heard.

Today we are covered in His righteousness and empowered to make our way toward Him in surrender. Muttered prayers of salvation or not, we know firsthand what it is to be saved.

God, today I choose not to trust in my own efforts, but to trust in the deep work You have done in my heart. Savior keep before my eyes the price You paid to redeem me. God, deepen my faith, not based upon my own wishes and desires, but in You and what Your will is. Let Your mercy fall upon me, God.

✝

Day 7: *Predestined in Love*

"Praise be to the God and Father of our Lord Jesus Christ, who has blessed us in the heavenly realms with every spiritual blessing in Christ. For he chose us in him before the creation of the world to be holy and blameless in his sight. In love he predestined us for adoption to sonship through Jesus Christ, in accordance with his pleasure and will." Ephesians 1:3–5.

Meditating on this scripture should give us an awe-inspiring, uncontainable excitement that God, the Creator of the universe chose us to be His adopted children. However, as children, so many of us experienced extreme disappointment and disillusionment from extreme abuse and/or abandonment, which has left a fiery pain deep in our bellies.

Some of us were raised in a church with all the do's and don'ts of the Christian life. We heard from the pulpit about the miserable furnace of hell stoked by God's wrath where we will cry out night and day, gnashing our teeth in the horrors of eternal damnation if we don't shape up. Alongside us in recovery are those who have never attended even one church service and yet have heard the mention of hell and are forewarned that God should certainly be avoided.

Whatever our past, God loves us and decided long ago that we belong to Him and no other. We've been so focused on the God who hates sin that we've totally missed the God whose love is far-reaching and incomparable! All we need to do is look up to the sky on a clear night and see each star and understand that every single separate star has been named by this amazing God whose love has no beginning and no end.

Working the Twelve-Steps is essential if we are to unwrap ourselves from shame and come to know that God loves us no matter what! Despite the lack of hair on our head, the wart on our nose, or the pimple on our chin, God loves us and claims us as His own. While we are faithless and feckless, God still longs for us to turn to Him.

We are grateful for this chance at life and must resist the old playmates and playgrounds that suck us back into addictive behaviors. Resisting the evil that pounds at our door, we remember that we are redeemed and called by name and reject the thoughts that we are doomed and hopeless.

Sometimes we may wonder "if only" we had been taught love and not the fire and brimstone of hell as children, we might not have succumbed to addiction. But these thoughts are no longer relevant because, while Satan may have planned our death, God planned our life! He chose us. He chose you.

God, help me remember all You have done for me. God, that I would be pleasing to you. I offer myself to You to be Your arms, hands, and feet to bring your light where there is darkness. Bind me in Your love.

Day 8: *Alert and Sober*

"Be alert and of sober mind [rendered in an earlier edition as 'self-controlled']. Your enemy the devil prowls around like a roaring lion looking for someone to devour. Resist him, standing firm in the faith, because you know that the family of believers throughout the world is undergoing the same kind of sufferings." 1 Peter 5:8–9.

Even to the fair-weather football fan, it is obvious that the players and coaches plot and plan for each game with a carefully thought-out strategy. They assess the strengths and weaknesses of the opponent and adjust the plays and players; and engage in psychological warfare to defeat the other team.

Prior to the game, the players must be disciplined and work their bodies with a trainer and eat foods that supply proper nutrients to create the stamina and strength needed to resist and overcome their opponent. As the battle ensues, we root for our favorite team. If they are defeated, we experience disappointment, perhaps even blame and hurl insults as our team goes from hero to loser in the short span of two to three hours.

While people who do not have addiction problems seem to start their day in blessed freedom, we begin ours by working to overcome the greatest struggle of our lifetime: *Addiction.* We have nearly been devoured by its forceful nature and pressed down by its heavy chains. But wrapped in the mercy of God, our lowest point of defeat became our first step on the road to victory!

It is precisely because we were struck down by addiction that we are now ready to yield to the enveloping warmth of God's presence and safety. Surrounded by His love, tucked neatly into His embrace, we begin to learn, listen, and follow the directions of people He has placed in our lives. This requires the willingness to listen to our mentors and sponsors like we would listen to the most seasoned of coaches.

We begin to read God's Word (the best playbook known to mankind) and apply His strategies. He shows us the schemes of our foe who wants nothing more than our return to active addiction. No longer are we unaware of how Satan uses our addiction and lays traps because God is showing us the way! We claim the promise that our God is greater than any evil force that can come against us. We are blessed, rescued, redeemed, protected, saved, and loved more than we can ever know. Christ died for our sins and even now powerfully and jealously protects and guards us.

God, today I will study Your Word and who You are and have always been. You have overcome the world and are victorious and have crushed Satan under Your feet. Let me feel You envelop me today. Let the confidence I have in You be perfected.

Day 9: *Everyday Miracles*

"Yet you desired faithfulness even in the womb; you taught me wisdom in that secret place. . . .. Create in me a pure heart, O God, and renew a steadfast spirit within me." Psalm 51:6, 10.

In order to begin the recovery process, we must be convinced that addiction has proven to be more powerful than our best efforts to control our use of substances. While the Twelve-Steps of Alcoholics Anonymous basic text refers primarily to alcohol, the Twelve-Steps can help people struggling with non-alcohol-related problems such as eating disorders, gambling, sex addictions, emotional problems, and co-dependency.

Personal experiences — like the one that follows — are shared and heard in the meeting rooms of the Twelve-Step programs all across the world: "I remember the exact moment over 29 years ago, when God spoke to my inmost (or secret) place. The message vibrating within my heart to begin the recovery process was placed there by God. I never would have come up with that one on my own!"

I was traveling in my car after meeting with my child's father to discuss transferring custody to him, with no provision of visitation between my daughter and me. I was utterly defeated. Looking up toward the sky, tears streaming down my face, I asked God what I should do. I asked God for help. Immediately a gentle voice inside my inmost place said, "Go to treatment." The truth, a renewal of sanity, overwhelmed me and I admitted my powerlessness and followed the call.

Testimonies mirroring this one are heard time and again and are the extreme evidence that our God is a God of miracles.

Miracles are a common everyday thing for our God. He is powerful, mighty, awesome, loving, compassionate and loves His struggling kids with a passion we cannot even fathom.

When we read the Bible and the witness of the accounts of Jesus raising the dead back to life, we know it is possible because we see the evidence all around us and hear the stories of redemption and resurrection every day.

Our experience is one of having been spiritually dead in addiction and being brought back to life in recovery. What a miracle that God has reached in and given to us the desire to steadfastly attend to His instruction and learn to hear His voice.

God, help me hear You today. Let my full being cry out to You and attend to Your will. God, that your truth would give me the ability to follow Your will, which is to always prosper and never harm me.

✝

Day 10: *The Underground of Humanity*

*"For You do not desire sacrifice, or else I would give it; you do not
delight in burnt offering. The sacrifices of God are a broken spirit, a
broken and a contrite heart – these, O God, You will not despise."*
Psalm 51:16–17.
(The New King's James Version)[3]

There is a unique fragility to our brokenness as we begin the
recovery process. Others cannot even begin to comprehend our
suffering and the old-timers in the program seem to have
forgotten. But the brokenhearted are often more open to the
presence of the Holy Spirit than an every-Sunday churchgoer
who has never stepped out of line their entire lives, except for
little "inconsequential" sins.

Addiction convinced us that our lives were broken beyond
repair – that we have been damaged by the things we have done.
They are so terrible we can barely admit to ourselves much less
admit to a pastor or other church member.

However, despite the complete and incomprehensible
demoralization we have experienced, in desperate faith we
turned to God and asked Him to comfort us in the midst of deep
guilt and shame. We had been reduced to living our lives in the
underground of humanity and realized that while it may be a
long way back into the good graces of society, we are only a
whisper away from the courts of God's grace.

Because of our great pain, and facing the threat of more, we
realized that there was nowhere else for us to turn but to Jesus
and the Twelve-Steps He laid at our feet. Turning to Jesus wasn't

---

[3] *The New King's James Version*, (Thomas Nelson; 2018)

because we woke up one day and thought it was a good idea to ask Him into our lives! No, we turned to Him because we lacked the power to survive our suffering and prevent more catastrophic events from happening. Driven by our pain, we sheepishly glanced in God's direction while immersed in the turmoil of shame. Amazed, hopeful, and astonished, we were grateful beyond all we had hoped for that Jesus gazed back at us and held out His hand.

God tells us it is in this heart-wrenching brokenness — the place where we lay it all down and no longer rely on our own human power — that He is well-pleased, and, in fact, delighted with us!

When we admit we cannot go on without Him and accept that we are broken and incomplete without His help, He does not despise our cry for help. Instead, He is elated that we have called on Him. The angels in heaven celebrate the pleas for help from this dear and beloved child of God and cheer as God reaches out and scoops us up into His presence.

God, today help me put aside any thoughts of self-reliance. God, let my heart break anew remembering the cry I made asking You for help so long ago. Let the cry of my heart be pleasing to You as I lay down all that I think I know and listen to the still small voice of Your loving Spirit.

✟

Day 11: *Pressing on Towards the Goal*

"Not that I have already obtained all this, or have already arrived at my goal, but I press on to take hold of that for which Christ Jesus took hold of me. . . .. Forgetting what is behind and straining toward what is ahead, I press on toward the goal." Philippians 3:12-14.

When we continue to dwell on our failures, we re-experience them over and over again, re-creating unwelcome thoughts of shame, conviction, regret, and defeat. The accuser tortures us as he pricks and prods at the most tender places of our hearts. He whispers that we're failures and will never succeed in recovery. He reminds us of how we failed as parents, sons, daughters, wives and husbands, and that we are beyond the healing and restorative power of God.

But the deepest desire in our hearts is to please and live out the will of our Father. We have been called by Jesus to live in the now and shake off the past and are encouraged to live in forgiveness.

There are times the lies of Satan will be louder than we can bear, and we may descend into self-will, depression and self-pity. However, with God's power, we are learning to recognize the cycle of despair and the refining fire of God's healing in our lives.

We hear often in meetings that time takes time and we don't become white as the driven snow just because we are clean and sober. But this isn't true for those who call out to Jesus! He has made us new and alive in the love and sacrifice poured out for us on the cross. We have been redeemed and right now where we sit or stand, we have been made perfect because Jesus gave His all for us at the cross.

God is not done with us and we will continue suffer through the change that is to come, but He will be there through it all. In active addiction, we were driven by our need to escape from reality.

Today, we have been relieved from the obsession, shame, and accusation levied at us by the evil one, because Jesus died so that we could live. He paid the price for every terrible and evil thing we have done in the past and will commit in the future. Because He lives, we are covered in His grace and tucked neatly in by God's love, which knows no beginning and will suffer no end.

God, today my heart hurts from the failures of the past. The accuser stands at the door of my mind pointing his accursed finger me. God, You know my heart. Relieve me of the burden I carry. Help me press in and turn my pain into joy.

Day 12: *Picking up Our Mats*

"One who was there had been an invalid for thirty-eight years. When Jesus saw him lying there and learned that he had in this condition for a long time, he asked him, 'Do you want to get well?'" John 5:5–6.

Just imagine lying in a ditch and after thirty-eight years of alcoholic torture, our friends bring Jesus to heal us. There would be no regret, no shame, and we would not dwell on the past! NO! We'd jump up and dance for joy, ready to live our lives to the full.

Many of us came to sobriety through the doors of a treatment center or the Twelve-Step program. Regardless of how we trudged over the threshold and into recovery, we can recall the still small voice that spoke us into motion. We jumped up and were willing to do almost anything to stop the pain that drove us to desperation. We heard God's call and felt hope stir new life into our hearts.

Our friends in recovery have told us what we need to do to stay sober. and we believe they are God-given instruments of healing in our lives. God has set our feet on a path designed just for us and is showing us one day at a time the way we should go. If we are willing to listen, we will hear our Lord's call of hope as He asks us if we wish to be made well.

Like the man at the pool, we are willing to pick up our mats, heed His call and surrender to His great and glorious will for our lives. Whatever our affliction might be, in the quiet still moment of today, Jesus' words hold great relevance for our lives as He asks, "Do you wish to get well?"

His words require us to honestly ask ourselves if we are willing to apply action to our daily lives by picking up our mats on the unknown path of recovery as we move away from sin and toward the Holiest of Holies.

Are we ready to stand up and shake off the terrors of yesterday and live in the miracle of today?

Lord, today I choose to be well – I choose Your healing hand. I desire You in my life today. God give me the strength and desire to pick up my mat and follow You all the days of my life – one day at a time.

Day 13: *The Riptide of Obsession*

*"For in the Gospel the righteousness of God is revealed – a
righteousness that is by faith from first to last, just as it is written:
'The righteous will live by faith.'"* Romans 1:17.

Our minds are foggy and it's hard to understand what it
means to live by faith! Life has collapsed in on us and we're sick
and tired of how we are living. As we contemplate change, we
feel fear, but pick up our mats and drag ourselves into recovery
anyway.

We're beginning to feel the stirring of hope in our hearts and
that small mustard seed of faith begins to take root. We know
God has heard our cries for help because there is no way we
would be where we are today without His supernatural
response to our prayer. He is the extravagant lover of our souls
and wants to perfect our faith in Him so we can be well.

Our faith continues to develop and grow each day as we
continue to walk toward Him. We're still not completely
convinced that He loves us, but those feelings will shift and
change like the tides of the ocean. So, we focus on living one day
at a time through riptides that often seem to overwhelm us and
pull us back into obsessive thinking.

God has told us that if we focus our eyes on Him and seek
His presence, He will be there to comfort, guide, and protect us.
He loves us—we are His dearly loved children. The pureness of
God's love for us sends the waves of faith crashing in to revive
us and wash away any fear or threat to our sobriety.

Freedom has come and we are no longer held captive to the
seduction of our addiction. God is mighty to save and has
overcome the evil lurking around us and patiently waiting to

destroy the work that God is doing in our lives. But we belong to God, and no power or principality can change that! Today we will live by faith—just because He said so.

God, today even though I may be in the midst of pain or experiencing loss, trauma, or heartache, let me remember You are in control. Remind me daily that I am set free from my addiction. God, let my eyes be on You and trust the tide will turn.

Day 14: *Perfect Weakness*

"He said to me, 'My grace is sufficient for you, for my power is made
perfect in weakness.' Therefore, I will boast all the more gladly about
my weaknesses, so that Christ's power may rest on me."
2 Corinthians 12::9.

The wisdom of the world tells us it is foolishness to admit defeat. You are a loser, weak, and a victim instead of a champion. Admitting powerlessness certainly does not fall in line with society's all-consuming preoccupation with social justice. The women's empowerment movement rebels against women admitting they are powerless and claim the Twelve-Steps are insensitive toward women who have been mistreated and abused by people more powerful or in positions of authority.

It is understandable for those who work with abused women or children to want them to be empowered, but they don't understand what Step One means. It is a blessing; Step One means we are welcomed and encouraged to lean upon a power greater than ourselves—a power so great that at the sound of His voice even the rocks cry out in worship! They don't understand that when we lay down our own power and lean into the power of God, we are safer than we have ever been or will ever be in our lives!

It is precisely because we are willing to admit defeat that God's power is ready to swoop in and set us free. As worldly wisdom cries foul and warns against giving up personal power, we turn from it and allow God to empower us to stay sober!

One day at a time we realize that we no longer find our healing in a bottle of booze, a fistful of pills or other substances. We realize that in order to grasp on to the power of God, we must lay down our own clever thinking, personal fables, and modern or ancient philosophies. While it defies common logic, we must admit that without God we are lost and hopeless. Our hearts are cracking open, and we feel God flowing in. How amazing it is to be in recovery and experience a new miracle every day.

God, today, help me put aside my pride. You are my savior, my redeemer, my refuge, and my friend. Calm the storms raging inside of my mind, body, and spirit. Help me rest in the knowledge You are in control, and I can let go.

✝

Day 15: *He Won't Ever Send Us Away!*

> *"Then Jesus called the children over to him and said to the disciples, 'Let the little children come to me! Never send them away! For the Kingdom of God belongs to men who have hearts as trusting as these little children's. And anyone who doesn't have their kind of faith will never get within the Kingdom's gates.'" Luke 18:16–17.*
> *(The Living Bible)*

It is hard to imagine a society where children weren't whisked off to music lessons, sports, and extra scholastic programs as they are today in our frenzied society. Sometimes, and sadly enough, even in our churches, addicts and alcoholics, the poor, children without parents, and the homeless who are desperately in need of a shower are similarly shunned and avoided except on holidays, church-sponsored special events, or missions.

This type of holiday compassion isn't unique to churches. Twelve-Step members aren't off the hook, because it isn't uncommon for us to look down our noses at others who continually relapse for years on end or haven't yet grasped the program. We treat them like they are losers and give up on them even in the midst of their struggles.

As a society of recovering people, we believe the newcomer, whether fresh off the street or a habitual relapsing member, is the most important person at the meeting. While they might still be struggling and resisting recovery, there is a beat-up and exhausted attitude of defeat and which surrender we can learn from. Compassion flows around the room as they talk about the terror of relapse.

However, we may also have judgmental thoughts at the same time because there must be some reason for their inability to stay sober! Our thoughts of judgment are usually present, because we have begun to believe that it is because of will-power that we are sober and take credit for our new-found or long-term recovery.

Our pride and self-deception will rob us of the joy of remembering that God scooped us up from the horror of our addiction and set us on our feet with His blessing just because we're His kids. He wants us to look up into His face with child-like joy because He values, loves, and cares for us.

Recovery is all about us becoming less and God becoming more as we pray for others to share in our blessings. As God's children, we are encouraged to come and enjoy His presence. No one can stop us.

God, today let the joy of all You have saved me from surround my heart with the blessing of salvation so that I might help others. God, help me see the struggling child beyond the resistive and closed heart embittered by addiction.

Day 16: *He was Tempted so He can Help*

"Because he himself suffered when he was tempted,
he is able to help those who are being tempted."
Hebrews 2:18.

There are so many memories of pain and disappointment, and we still feel like we're alone and no one understands. We think God doesn't care or understand our pain, longing, and suffering because we don't really know quite yet who He is.

Dwelling on the terrible things we have done to ourselves and to others, we think God can never forgive us or change our lives and we're so tired of feeling sad and hopeless! These thoughts and feelings come upon us when we least expect them, and we want nothing more than to be free from the feelings of hopelessness, aloneness, abandonment, depression, grief, or loss.

Sometimes we want to club ourselves over the head because we can't control when they come and when they go! Immersed in the pit of self-obsession, our addiction begins to stir up and re-emerge, taking over once again. This is a natural phase of our recovery because we are human, and there is no way around it — only through it.

Our God is merciful, and we need only call out to Him. He waits patiently, lovingly, and longingly for us to turn to Him. God is not passive. He is a there in times of trouble and understands completely what it is to have physical pain, emotional turmoil, and feelings of intense rejection.

Jesus was spat upon, beaten, tortured, and despised. He experienced more pain than any human can know; His own

47

Father turned away from Him as He hung there on the cross cloaked in our sin!

He wants us to know that we are understood, loved, and valued. Only He offers us complete understanding, love, and acceptance. Addiction can offer only an illusory, temporary sense of relief followed by incomprehensible demoralization. The greatest temptation we will face is turning way from God! Instead, we focus our eyes on Him and look to His grace.

God, You know my pain and suffering, and You know what brings joy. Let me take hope and courage in You and realize that my circumstances are temporary. My hope is in You, Jesus.

✝

Day 17: *Created, Redeemed and Adopted*

"Justification by grace through faith means that I know myself
accepted by God as I am. When my head is enlightened and my heart
is pierced by this truth, I can accept myself as I am. It is an act of faith
in the God of Grace."[4]

As we attend meetings and listen to those who have gone
before us, it begins to dawn on us that somehow and
mysteriously the all-consuming thoughts of self-hatred have left
us. We have suffered profound losses because drugs and
alcohol, or food and gambling ruled our lives. They harmed our
bodies and impaired our ability to think, reason, feel, and
engage in meaningful relationships. Our hearts were hurt, and
our innocence was smashed by the weight of eroded self-esteem
and self-acceptance.

Addiction drove us to do terrible things and robbed us of
the ability to experience real, rather than manufactured, joy. But
recovery is showing us a new way to live with purpose and
meaning stirring in our hearts. We have an inkling of hope and
are beginning to believe that we might be able to do this thing!

There are even times we can exhale a sigh of relief as a
weight of regret rolls off our hearts, because no longer are we
the tornado that tore apart lives. We are a new creation and
dearly loved by our Savior who snatched us from the grip of
darkness. Jesus lives in us and tangles on a daily basis with —
and reigns victorious over — our addiction, empowering us with
God's strength. By the power of the cross, we are forgiven —
completely and utterly white as snow!

---

[4] Brennan Manning, *Ragamuffin Gospel*, (Multnomah, 2005) *p. 49.*

Even though we hear in the rooms that this is a process or progress rather than perfection, we know the truth. Sometimes it's hard to believe that we are unconditionally loved by God just the way we are—every hidden and haunted corner of our being. Jesus gave His life for us so we could overcome our incessant thoughts of hopelessness and despair.

It is impossible to feel anything else but gratitude when we acknowledge that He died for us and rose again so that we could know we are loved and fully accepted by God exactly as we are right now, in this moment.

God, let my heart know the fullness of Your love. God, let my response to Your love be an acceptance of myself as Your created, redeemed, and adopted child. God, help me experience the extravagant love of who You are and always remember it is enough.

✝

Day 18: *Biting the Hand of Those Who Help*

"Trust God from the bottom of your heart; don't try to figure out everything on your own. Listen for God's voice in everything you do, everywhere you go; he's the one who will keep you on track. Don't assume that you know it all. Run to God! Run from evil! Your body will glow with health, your very bones will vibrate with life!"
Proverbs 3:5–6
(The Message)

Is it any wonder alcoholics, addicts, and al-anon's alike are dragged kicking, sometimes screaming and biting the hand of those who are trying to help? Delusions of self-sufficiency have made us think we can do this all on our own—that we have everything under control, thank you very much![5]

We bristle at the notion that we need any help from anyone to help us overcome the grip addiction has had over us. After all, the people who need help are losers, weak and cannot change anyway. We're not like them! We're certainly not ready to admit that we need a power greater than ourselves to keep us sober (we're not there yet!).

Instead we try to find relief in a new pair of shoes, a new car, a triple-stacked cheeseburger, or a new romantic relationship. But this relief is temporary, and we realize it is a throwaway approach to life that in the end causes harm because we care more about ourselves and couldn't care less about others.

We may find ourselves flipping people off as we drive down the freeway, yelling at the checker in the grocery store,

---

[5] Alcoholics Anonymous, *Twelve Steps and Twelve Traditions*, (AA World Services; 2002), pg. 21.

verbally accosting the panhandler on the side of the street, or leaving the raising of our children to others because we're too busy raging in the temper of self-obsession.

When we immerse ourselves in addictive and destructive behaviors, we reject the beauty God longs to create in our hearts. Recovery requires that we stop engaging in destructive behaviors so we can claim the freedom and hope of change. Recovery will evade us if we continue to cling to old behaviors and ignore God's truth (Proverbs 3:5–6).

We must admit complete defeat and raise our flags in surrender and ask God to forgive us for abandoning His truth in favor of our own. The thought of surrendering ourselves to God may fill us with fear, but we have tried everything else known to man and seen the results. But we are willing to continue the journey and wade our way through fear because we're beginning to believe that maybe, just maybe, Jesus is where the foundation of trust, truth, and eternity are found.

God, today let my natural instinct of willful self-sufficiency be replaced by the willingness to listen to You and to others. Let me lay down at Your feet my own understanding as You fill me anew and make straight my path in recovery.

✝

Day 19: *He is Faithful, Kind and Dependable*

"All of you, clothe yourselves with humility toward one another,
because, God opposes the proud but shows favor to the humble.
Humble yourselves, therefore, under God's mighty hand, that he may
lift you up in due time. Cast all your anxiety on him
because he cares for you." 1 Peter 5:5–7.

Lives torn into tatters — ripped wide open — with our heads hung in shame for the things we have done, humiliated and unworthy, we finally enter through the doors of the Twelve-Step program. We feel as though we just can't go on anymore and are afraid to admit to others how desperate we feel.

It is not unusual for us to recognize the thoughts of suicide roaming around loose in our minds and try as we might we cannot control these unwelcome invading thoughts of desperation. Pain permeates our hearts, and we feel powerless to stop the pain and change the chaos and disorder. We are told to pray, wait, reach out to others, and talk to other recovering people who have gone before us and experienced exact same feelings and thoughts.

Crushed, beaten, and soul-less is how we feel, and we struggle to believe others are telling us the truth that this is *not* how our lives will always be. We hear over and over again that "this too shall pass."

These times of desperation are often what it takes for "our kind" to be brought to our knees and become willing to seek recovery in the Twelve-Steps. Thankfully our God is gracious and brings us into His presence so we can rest our heads on His shoulder and cast our anxieties on Him.

We are amazed and can hardly believe that as we rest in His presence, our anxieties recede, and we feel the love of God provide a balm of comfort over our hearts and minds. These moments of intimacy might not last for long periods of time, but they are beautiful and unforgettable.

In those moments we are free from the thoughts of old, no longer stuck in the loop of depression, anxiety, or hopelessness. When we close our eyes and rest in His presence, we will find that He is faithful, kind, dependable, and true.

God, today let me experience Your care, Your kindness. Let me shake off the lie that You are mad at me, displeased because of what I have done. Help me know that all is forgiven, and I am loved.

✝

Day 20: *Blessed in Hopelessness*

"Blessed are the poor in spirit, for theirs is the kingdom of heaven.
Blessed are those who mourn, for they shall be comforted. Blessed are
the gentle, for they shall inherit the earth. Blessed are those who
hunger and thirst for righteousness, for they shall be satisfied.
Matthew 5:3–6
(The New American Standard Version)[6]

How can it be that hopeless and helpless addicts are blessed? We certainly fit the profile of being poor in spirit, because we mourn for all we lost and feel so awful about ourselves, because we have hurt so many people! We have been beat down, despised, and rejected because of our addiction and have become acutely aware of how our addiction impacted the lives of those we love.

However, we still can't shake the tendency to blame others and find the victim hat still perfectly fits as we try to escape the feelings of guilt and avoid responsibility. Pointing our finger at others, politics, or societal rules, we blame everyone and everything for our suffering and because we lack humility.

We rail at the world. If it would change, we would be fine! Maybe we blame the liberal or conservative agenda, or the fact that men make more money than women, or all white people are prejudiced and have better luck than everyone else.

The truth is that life is unfair, people can be hostile and dangerous, and stuff happens! However, our addiction has twisted our thinking and takes the unfairness of life and uses it

---

[6] *New American Standard Version*, (Foundation Publications, Inc. Anaheim, CA. 1998.)

to make excuses for our own poor behavior and consequences therein.

But Step One shows us that beneath the layers of shame and the endless stream of excuses, we find that admitting powerlessness over things beyond our control becomes our greatest strength. Our deep regrets often foster our need to control things and drive us to despair. This is why we don't regret our past or shut it out!

Relinquishing control is actually becoming meek, and we find God is ever-present and able to break through the chains of bondage. He is willing and able to do what we have never been able to do on our own. In the quiet corners of our spirit, God is already preparing us for the harvest of His blessings. The rushing and healing waters of God will wash away our pain and suffering! He is filling us with hope that the promise of freedom will come.

God, thank You for Your promise that even though I fear being overcome by my grief and loss, You are there to comfort me. Father, if I must break to heal, let the fractures of my heart become the wellsprings of Your promise.

Day 21: *We See the Light*

"No one lights a lamp and puts it in a place where it will be hidden, or under a bowl. Instead they put it on its stand, so that those who come in may see the light." Luke 11:33.

It may be hard to believe, but there will come a day when we will look back on our early recovery as an exciting and miraculous time in our lives. We realize that it was supernatural how all of a sudden we awakened, aware and able to think clearly for the first time in many years.

Finally, we are free from the agonizingly intense cravings and crazy thoughts. Our hearts feel light and our minds are free from the constant obsessive thoughts of self-contempt. No longer controlled by confusion, pain, and suffering, we are grateful to have been plucked from the misery and intense degradation caused by active addiction.

Despite our tendency to be thickheaded, there is not a shred of doubt that this is the work of a power greater than us, and we want to dance with hope (but we're kind of scared to become too hopeful!). God is beginning a work in us so we can enjoy sobriety and learn to let God in more and more.

We do spend a lot of time whining and complaining as newbies in recovery but thank God our sponsors can help guide us through the process. As the light of the Spirit of God comes in, the darkness and confusion have no other option but to flee. What a joy it is to realize that we don't need to live in darkness any longer or be alone!

There is no shame in needing other people to help guide us in our recovery, and we are learning day by day to trust. As we begin to acclimate ourselves to this new way of life we realize that God uses others to help us navigate our way through early recovery.

God is encouraging us to travel close to Him as He shows us the way. And it is a relief to realize that we will continue to change because God loves us too much to leave us like we are! For now, we will continue on, step by step, and do the next right indicated thing.

God, today let my light shine bright. Illuminate the dark recesses of my mind, body, and spirit and chase out anything that would block me from You.

Day 22: *Tripping on Sin*

"It happens so regularly that it's predictable. The moment I decide to do good, sin is there to trip me up. I truly delight in God's commands, but it's pretty obvious that not all of me joins in that delight. Parts of me covertly rebel, and just when I least expect it, they take charge.
Romans 7:21–23
(*The Message*)

We're misfits and losers—and yet at the same time we believe we are helpless and hapless victims. We are walking-talking contradictions!

These thoughts are a recipe for failure for the recovering person and can cause us to sink fast into further rebellion. We feel powerless and hopeless. It seems as though nothing we've done has ever been good enough, and we burn inside because we think nothing will ever change and we'll always be who we've always been!

But it is important that we don't throw in the towel and quit. We have thought this way for a very long time, and while, yes, we are in recovery, it takes time for these self-destructive thoughts to change. Our friends in recovery will help us learn to think in ways that don't feed into our addiction.

We are realizing that our minds have been overcome by this horrible disease that brought such wreckage to our lives and swept up everyone we loved or cared about into the same painful pit. Step One helps us see that our addiction began with our rebellion against society's rules and biblical truths. We packed up and pushed on in our quest for comfort, excitement, fun, enlightenment, and relevance. We wanted what we wanted when we wanted it!

Initially, this land of happiness made us feel whole, complete, and worthy of everything the world had to offer. Rebellion wasn't painful! It was fun and rewarding! We knew better than everyone else and flaunted how amazing our lives were. Hooray for me—screw you!

Until—and this day came fast—we lost the ability to control the fallout of rebellion and it turned on us. We were powerless to break free and were frustrated beyond belief finding ourselves doing things we didn't want to do! Unable to extricate ourselves from the powerful grip of addiction no matter what we tried or attempted to do, we were thrust deeper into the cycle of despair.

But today we are grateful for Step One as God shows us that His grace has the power to help us overcome our addiction. Today we accept that even though we will trip, God will never let us fall.

God, today I commit myself to You. Today, I am not the victim under the powerful force of addiction. I am an overcomer, a glorified, loved, and cherished child of God.

✝

Day 23 *No Longer Condemned*

"There is now no condemnation for those who are in Christ Jesus, because through Christ Jesus the law of the Spirit who gives life set has set you free from the law of sin and death." Romans 8:1–2.

Early in recovery as we set a course for our faith walk with Jesus, we tend to think of the law as something created by the "perfect people" of society—you know the ones who just don't know what fun is!

If we went to church as kids, we may have heard about the Ten Commandments or other laws in the Bible that were impossible for us to keep. Many of us were forced to attend a Twelve-Step program because we were arrested by the police, charged by the prosecutor, and then sentenced by a judge. This wasn't our idea of fun!

On the tails of our legal troubles, our lives are a mess and we beat ourselves up, and even if we haven't gone to church before, we know this isn't how decent people live. There is something not right about us and we can't seem to pinpoint what the problem is. We do know that we're either on one side of the law or the other: upholding and obeying or breaking and disobeying.

Of course, we've been on the wrong side—for a long time! This has resulted in going to jail, losing our kids, or being shunned by the law-abiders! It has also led to a lifetime of incarceration or even being condemned to death. Breaking God's laws also has life-altering consequences.

Regardless of where our law-breaking has brought us, it is God's laws that free us rather than condemn us. He has set us free from our sick and twisted behaviors and everything that haunts us. Even though people have given up on us, God hasn't, and He never will! Our God is compassionate, loving, righteous, and true! His law is good for us and gives life instead of death!

Wherever we are and whatever we are facing, God is for us and wants to make us well. Today, let us remember that our greatest gift is forgiveness.

God, let me rejoice in my innermost being that You have set me free from the bondage of self! God, when the negative thoughts of self-condemnation overtake me and strike my heart, let me remember all You have done for me.

Day 24: *The Thirst for Change*

"Defeat does not come to those who trust in you, but to those who are quick to rebel against you. Teach me your ways, O Lord; make them known to me. Teach me to live according to your truth, for you are my God, who saves me. I always trust in you. Remember, O Lord, your kindness and constant love which you have shown from long ago. Forgive the sins and errors of my youth. In your constant love and goodness, remember me, Lord! Psalm 25:3–7

(Good News Translation)[7]

What wondrous, healing, and life-changing words these are for those of us who thirst for change! Regardless of how our rebelliousness began, we have real turmoil in our lives! There is so much rot and decay in our lives because of our addiction. We've tried hard to keep our eyes tightly shut and not see how our choices put into motion our discontentment, pain, and a never-ending appetite for more.

With the need for instant gratification, we were either unaware or didn't care about the pain we inflicted on our unfortunate victims. Not only did we harm those who were close to us, we also hurt people we didn't know by stealing from them or driving under the influence and unleashing a 4,000-pound weapon in their lives.

When we think about it, first we may shudder, but then we are overcome with gratitude that we're not like that anymore! God is transforming us and has given us a teachable and contrite spirit. Today we thirst for what is good and righteous. Ready

---

[7] *Good News Translation*, (Zondervan; 2001)

and willing, we ask God to show us what we cannot see and give us what we need to make it one more day.

We seek God with the desperation of a dying man who wants to live and see his children grow-up. We groan inside because of what we've done in the past, but when guilt threatens to overwhelm us, God's forgiveness comforts us. We may still struggle with flashes of the things we have done, so it is important that we remember that we are loved, forgiven, and found worthy because Jesus made it so!

Our baggage may still trip us up, but God is always there to catch us, pick us up and dust us off. We are learning to trust Him and open ourselves up more to learn what He wants to teach us.

God, today I ask for the continued desire to stay clean and sober. If there is anything I am doing that will prevent my journey toward You, please remove it! Remember me in Your loving kindness.

Day 25: *Swept up in Peace, Joy, Certitude and Love*

"At some point we were deeply touched by a profound encounter with Jesus Christ. It was a mountaintop experience, a moment of immense consolation. We were swept up in peace, joy, certitude, love. We were deeply moved for a few hours, days or weeks."[8]

As we make ourselves available to the recovery process and one-day-at-a-time living, we are captivated by the thought that we can live happy and wholesome lives like our recovery friends! We start to realize how God is softly and subtly nudging our hearts to become willing to change.

Hard as it may be to believe, the crushing experience that brought us to recovery was meeting Jesus on that mountaintop. He reached out and pulled us up and set our feet on solid ground. We know there was nothing we did to save ourselves and know that He is responsible for this new chance at life.

We're starting to think that maybe, just maybe, we're ready for this "coming to believe" in Step Two. Maybe God does want what is best for us and has thought enough about us to have an actual plan for our lives. One thing is for sure, recovery has altered our lives.

We encountered God on a bridge as we contemplated killing ourselves or behind the wheel of our car as we thought of ramming ourselves into a guardrail. This is our mountaintop! Wherever we were, God spoke to our hearts and rescued us.

He may have whispered in our hearts that we should go to treatment, or go to meetings, or call our pastor and ask for help. However, He communicated to us, we know without a doubt if

---

8 Manning, *Ragamuffin Gospel*, p. 178.

He hadn't extended grace, our lives would have continued on to the bitter end of destruction. We've been chewed up and spit out by our addiction time after time, abandoned, persecuted, and crushed after thirteen or more aborted or completed treatment attempts. Regardless of the twists and tangles of our recovery process, God has moved us by His own hand and profoundly touched our lives.

His call, although inaudible, was heard somewhere deep in our hearts as the gentle whisper of God called to us in the tenor of love asking us to depend on Him and listen. Awestruck, we realize that God has given us the will to live and a hope we have never had before. We are not alone, and while we might be powerless, God is able to powerfully take our mustard-seed-sized faith and move the mountains of hurt, rejection, pain, and suffering and restore our lives.

God, let my mountaintop experience remain fresh in my heart. Your faith is always inside my heart. Lord, let Your love settle in my heart and help me be strengthened by your spirit. Let me be rooted in Your love.

Day 26: *Learning to Sit and Hurt*

"I pray that out of his glorious riches he may strengthen you with power through his Spirit in your inner being, so that Christ may dwell in your hearts through faith. And I pray that you, being rooted and established in love, may have power, together with all the Lord's holy people, to grasp how wide and long and high and deep is the love of Christ, and to know this love surpasses knowledge – that you may be filled to the measure of all the fullness of God." Ephesians 3:16–19.

The withdrawal symptoms of nightmares, tremors, diarrhea, vomiting, insomnia, paralyzing anxiety, depression, or even hallucinations are common in our early days of recovery. We beg God to remove our desire to use and stop this suffering! We know how to fix this pain, but we don't want to go through this again.

Once the intense withdrawals stop, we know it would be sheer insanity to pick up another substance and repeat the withdrawal process again. While we realize this has been horrifically painful, we also can see how our suffering brought us to the tender place where we sought out God to help us.

We can see the way He heard our call and helped us through the difficulties of early recovery. Today, we live in a time where allowing people to suffer withdrawal is seen as cruel punishment, and the medical community is ready and able to write a prescription for our endless physical complaints.

While we do not need to be martyrs, we need to be *painfully* honest with ourselves and others! Most professionals trying to help us don't fully understand the addiction that drives us and wants to kill us. They have a heart to help and sometimes it is to our detriment.

The pharmaceutical companies enthusiastically create, manufacture and deliver legal drugs to replace the illegal ones. Yet, we're the ones who choose to accept the prescriptions!

We are not social justice warriors and it is none of our business what the medical community or pharmaceutical companies do. Our responsibility is to be painstakingly honest with ourselves and be willing to suffer for a little while and learn to sit and hurt.

Our strength and power come through the cross and God promises we will not suffer alone. When addiction, withdrawal, or life batters us, and we suffer deep and agonizing pain, God is there and will strengthen us with His power.

God, today let me rest in Your love that I cannot even begin to comprehend. As deep and wide as the ocean, and as high as the sky, Your love is everlasting and all-consuming. Might I experience just a portion of Your love today.

✞

Day 27: *Slow to Anger and Rich in Love*

"The Lord is gracious and compassionate, slow to anger and rich in love. The Lord is good to all; he has compassion on all he has made."
Psalm 145:8–9.

Grief, trauma, and loss are overwhelming feelings and it is frustrating when we continue to experience them even when we're sober! These feelings twist us and turn us inside out and we can't depend any longer on the instant relief we found in substances!

Sometimes we don't know if we can go on as the traumatic memories of childhood churn over and over in our minds. How could a God who is supposed to be so rich in mercy and slow to anger allow us to have gone through such trauma as kids?

Some of us were raised in families that went to church every Sunday, or maybe we spent four days a week in religious services. For the life of us we can't understand how God could have let us go astray and make such a mess of our lives!

Or, maybe we never set foot in a church and were still exposed to harmful abuse or devastating neglect and are equally dumbfounded that this "loving God" could have let this happen to us! These are all valid questions and feelings that we will get to in time.

However, Step One tells us that we must remain in today as the stage is set for God to reveal Himself to us and fill the gigantic hole in our gut. Some of us are mad at God and think of Him as a shallow grave-dwelling spirit with the primary goal of punishing our wayward souls.

Most likely we will learn in the coming days of our recovery that we never really knew who God was. Along with the rest of

69

our youth group, we may have been threatened with being "left behind." No dancing, dating, swearing, kissing, hand-holding, or any kind of provocative behavior was to be tolerated or God would be displeased and hasten our way into everlasting darkness. Our God was one of rules and condemnation.

But God is good, and through our recovery He is opening us up and teaching us about His all-consuming compassion, grace, and love. He is slow to anger and rich in love; instead of punishing us for our past transgressions, He is sweeping us up into His healing presence.

God, help me realize the love and forgiveness You have so richly blessed me with. There is nothing I did to earn Your love and nothing I can do to lose Your love. Let me put to rest the god of my youth, the god of intense anger and judgment and cling to Your garment of love.

✝

Day 28: *The Beauty of Brokenness*

"To be alive is to be broken. And to be broken is to stand in need of grace. There is a beautiful transparency to honest disciples who never wear a false face and do not pretend to be anything but who they are."[9]

People in the church may live their whole lives and never experience the painful beauty of brokenness. We're told that good Christians don't have problems! But the truth is that good Christians do have problems — we just hide them.

Despite our turmoil, we put on the Sunday game face to hide the reality that our husband is an adulterer; our children are on drugs; or we've lost our home through bankruptcy. Or it may be that we have been sexually abused, physically accosted by our spouse, or are suffering from an eating disorder, or a drug, sex, alcohol or gambling addiction.

Instead of sharing our burdens, we're afraid that our friends will know the truth that somehow God skipped over our house when bestowing the blessings of this life. Somehow, we began to think that we have to be perfect to be accepted.

Megachurches have sprung up everywhere with worship bands that imitate the famous by having only young, beautiful, and perfect people on stage. Music is beneficial and allows the Word of God and the Spirit of Christ to collide within us and bring a beautiful and worshipful experience.

But we have learned to take the good with the bad and remember that it is not our right to judge! In fact, we veer far away from taking a worship band or church's inventory! We're

---

[9] Manning, *Ragamuffin Gospel*, pg. 85.

broken and already have enough on our plates. Our goal is to be, open-minded and willing, because God likes us weaklings! When we're weak He is strong. Period.

We openly admit we are a wreck and our lives are unmanageable. Yes, we are a living, breathing and divine mess, but God is healing us and bringing us to the very edge of belief!

God, today let me remember my brokenness and face life with the transparency that comes from living in the truth of my circumstances, be they good or bad. Let me acknowledge the blessings that have come from pain and remember in the midst of suffering that You are there in the glory of my heart.

Day 29: *Loving One Another*

"Dear friends, let us love one another, for love comes from God.
Everyone who loves has been born of God and knows God. This is
love: not that we loved God, but that he loved us and sent his Son as
an atoning sacrifice for our sins. Dear friends, since God so loved us,
we also ought to love one another." 1 John 4:7, 10, 11.

Love doesn't come easily to us, but judgment does—and we judge ourselves harshly! Harsh judgment negatively impacts our recovery and decreases the likelihood of sustained and long-term recovery. This is why the steps are so important.

We are deeply distracted by resentments, yet at the same time feel immense shame and guilt about what we have done to others. While it may be easier to have thoughts of resentment and anger toward others for what they have done, our own guilt and shame percolates underground with the power to drive our actions and impede our progress in recovery.

Early recovery is difficult, and we are not yet ready to work Step Four where we look at our resentments or Steps Six and Seven where we acknowledge our defects of character. So, until then, we must learn to be gentle with ourselves and others and become ready to forgive.

It does not come easily or naturally to us to be kind to ourselves, and we have a hard time being kind to others who have hurt us. Twelve-Step meetings are a place where we love each other into wellness. Support, comradery, and hugs are the ingredients that help us learn patience because time takes time.

It is inspiring as we see young people give the elderly rides to meetings or the grocery store. We are inspired as we see the old helping young people navigate their way through the world as they learn to balance their first bank account, rent their first apartment, or learn how to shop in a grocery store.

The program embodies the love, true friendship, and discipleship fostered by the Spirit of Christ. "There is a nut for every screw" is a favorite saying in meetings, and in the eyes of the world, we may not be a successful lot, but we have learned how to love each other.

While we may not know it, the fellowship and brotherhood of suffering has brought us close to God. For the most part, we are a ragtag group of people from every corner of society holding onto each other for dear life! Driven to our knees in surrender, we are learning to love people we never would have met if not for our common problem.

Call it sin, call it whatever, but we have come together for a purpose and it doesn't matter what has driven us to our knees. We know that without the love for each other and the love of God, we would die a horrible, sad death.

God, thank You for being who You are: Love. Because of Your love, we can love each other. God, I pray for the church. May the gift of love AA has become manifested in the body of Christ.

✝

Day 30: *Drawing Close to God*

"But he gives us more and more strength to stand against all such evil longings. As the Scripture says, God gives strength to the humble but sets himself against the proud and haughty. So, give yourselves humbly to God. Resist the devil and he will flee from you. And when you draw close to God, God will draw close to you." James 4:6–8.
(*The Living Bible*)

Step One prepares us to accept the powerless and unmanageability of our addiction and then fills us with the reality that we need a power greater than ourselves if we are to survive, change, and grow in our recovery. We have come to know the insanity of our addiction and identified the thousands of ways we deceive ourselves.

If we just drink on weekends or only special occasions, or not mix pot with alcohol, meth with cocaine or with heroin, we might be successful in our drug use. I can eat the whole gallon of ice cream today and just not eat at all tomorrow and not gain weight. Or I can just play the penny slots at the casino and not blackjack so I don't lose as much money. We know all too well the overwhelming dishonesty of such thinking, but knowledge isn't enough to prevent our next relapse into active addiction.

Step One is coming to recognize that the evil one is tapping on our shoulder with the promise of, "Hey, you can do this and feel better! Remember when you (insert preference here) and the cares of the world lessened and you felt good, alive, calm and happy?" We might remember for a few moments how everyone wanted to be around us when we had drugs or money and were the life of the party. Seldom do we remember—until it is too late—that we were so loaded we ended up in embarrassing situations or so full of junk food we puked all over ourselves instead of in the toilet because we'd lost control of our vomit response.

Surrender is a great and glorious gift and we are grateful Step One has brought us face to face with our need for God. We realize now that being knocked upside the head was necessary to wake us up. There is no doubt that temptation will come, and the evil one wants nothing more than our failure. We are convinced that our success in recovery is in direct proportion to our willingness to submit to our Father in prayer and our hoped-for desire to experience the powerful blessing of recovery.

God, thank You for claiming me as Your own, and while I haven't enjoyed these painful times, I am grateful that You help me learn the lessons You have for me so that I can resist the evil one who seeks to destroy me. God, help me remember You are here, You are real, and that you are not a tempter but a deliverer. You are a God of compassion, of order and love.

Step Two

"Came to believe that a power greater than ourselves could restore us to sanity."
Alcoholics Anonymous

Day 1: *Coming to Believe*

"The law is good, then, and the trouble is not there but with me because I am sold into slavery with Sin as my owner. I don't understand myself at all, for I really want to do what is right, but I can't. I do what I don't want to — what I hate. I know perfectly well that what I am doing is wrong, and my bad conscience proves that I agree with these laws I am breaking. But I can't help myself because I'm no longer doing it. It is sin inside me that is stronger than I am that makes me do these evil things." Romans 7:14–17.
(The Living Bible)

We are living examples of this scripture because we have been slaves to our addiction and held against our will. Countless times we have tried to escape the devastating and morally degrading nature of our addiction, but our attempts have ended in failure. Despite trying to hide the shame churning inside of us, we lost relationships, children, jobs, and self-respect.

But we tried our very best to control the force that was within us and attempted to hide our addiction to save our reputation or marriage. The subversive and powerful nature of addiction continued to taunt and baffle us, and the enemy continued to lure us in so he could rob us of our very breath. There had been no shortage of attempts to fight, but we realized that we were at war with a power that was much more powerful than we were!

We tried cutting down on our use of food and control the use of other substances and made promised ourselves that this time would be different. This time we would only use alcohol instead of meth, or meth instead of alcohol. Whatever we tried to substitute, one for another, we were completely powerless.

We begged God to intervene and give us the power we so desperately needed to stay sober, clean or abstain from that next trip to a fast-food restaurant. Flesh and blood, caught in a tangled web of temptation, we tried to ward off the gigantic beast that seemed to have the power to best us at every turn no matter how hard we fought.

How did this happen again? We awaken numb or to tattered emotions, feelings of depression and hopelessness. Yet even as the enemy strikes and nicks us where it hurts, recovery equips us to fight back. The Twelve-Steps give us the opportunity to see how the addiction operates and how we can pray our way out of darkness and into the light.

Step Two is showing us a strategy of offense instead of having to constantly be on the defense. God is providing us with so many opportunities to learn about Him so we can speak God's truth when we are being attacked. The evil one may have power over our addiction; however, God is powerful and mighty and has already crushed Satan under His heel!

There is little doubt now that we need a power greater than ourselves to defend, protect, and free us from the chains of our addiction. We are coming to believe the importance and reality that we have an advocate who takes up our cause — Jesus Christ, the Righteous (1 John 2:1).

God, today help me see how the enemy tries to defeat me. God, let me claim the truth that You are there to shield me as I recover from this illness. Father, You are my defender, the holder of my head. No weapons formed against me will prosper (Isaiah 54:17).

✟

80

Day 2: *Blessed and Poor*

"Blessed are the poor in spirit, for theirs is the kingdom of heaven."
Matthew 5:3

A.W. Tozer well understood the blessedness of the poor in spirit. "The blessed ones . . . have repudiated every external thing. They have reached an inward state paralleling the outer circumstances of the common beggar. This is what the word 'poor' as Christ used it actually meant. These blessed poor are no longer slaves to the tyranny of things."

Many dedicate their entire lives to helping the poor in spirit, afflicted, and destitute rise up out of the pit of addiction: judges, attorneys, doctors, therapists, social workers, mentors, pastors, and elders spend countless hours and years and decades pouring out their hearts to prevent our death and help us live healthy and hopeful lives. Try as they might, most of our devoted helpers don't understand how important desperateness is to our healing process. It is only through desperation that we can contemplate surrender.

The condition we suffer from is grave and falling flat on our faces may be necessary so we can rise up on bended knee. In order for us to believe a power greater than ourselves can deliver us from the brink of madness, we must first see and feel to the full the crazy, incomprehensible, and demoralizing lived experience of addiction.

To become spiritual beggars is a gift and not something we need to be saved from! Maybe sleeping in our car—if we own one—in the dead of winter will help us reflect on the help we were offered or the treatment we received but didn't apply. That reflection may help us begin to hate how we are living. Only smashing and obliterating our pride can release us from bondage and set us free from the chains of addiction.

Step Two helps us turn away from the world's medicine cabinet, slot machines, kitchen cupboards, internet pornography, casinos, and nightclubs. We are convinced these "entertainments" poison our souls and do not eradicate the pain that gnaws away at our happiness. Moving forward into the gift of our recovery, we realize the painful circumstances have made us willing to contemplate God's will.

However, it is not the exercise of rejecting the material things of this world that will make us worthy; rather, it is the freedom we experience as we reject and turn from the sin of self-gratification. Finally, we know that only the Spirit of Christ can supply us with what we really need. We sink to our knees with our eyes focused on Him as we wait for Him with the hope of a panhandler.

God, today let me be alive in the freedom of Your Spirit! Thank You for all the circumstances that have left me empty and full of despair. It is because of these life situations and my failures that I can acknowledge I am poor and needy and only You can make me whole. I have found richness in You and a love found nowhere else. Blessed indeed are the poor in Spirit, for we know You.

Day 3: *God Is and God Can*

"It's impossible to please God apart from faith. And why? Because anyone who wants to approach God must believe both that he exists and that he cares enough to respond to those who seek him."
Hebrews 11:6
<small>(The Message)</small>
Suggested Reading: *Twelve Steps and Twelve Tradition's, pg. 28*

It's mind-boggling how much we struggle with the concept of coming to believe that a power greater than ourselves can and will restore us to sanity and relieve our suffering as we drag ourselves along the road of recovery.

The struggle is usually due to our past failed attempts of turning our lives over to God after joining several churches but never feeling like we fit in. Maybe after a pastor, counselor, or elder called our attention to our alcohol, drug, gambling, or pornography addictions, we were burned up—sore and angry that they would even dare to think such disgusting things about us. Fully convinced religion wasn't going to work for us—ever—we left our places of worship in a huff, dragging our loved ones with us and ignoring their spiritual needs. Maybe we washed our hands of the whole religion thing and let the family attend church alone. Raising our eyes to the heavens we told God, "thank you very much, but church just isn't for me."

So, we were going to go about this alone because people had failed and sinned against us. We burned inside with bruised egos, because we were left out of church leadership, not invited to social events, or were approached by elders about our bad behaviors. They had the nerve to call us out on our bad actions, and we grew resentful because other people did worse things!

83

But as our addiction progressed and our pride was smashed, we became convinced that we could not make a go of sobriety on our own and needed God's help. Perhaps it is this grasping and grappling experience of realizing our way doesn't work that makes us willing to try something else so we can experience a healthy and flourishing recovery.

Still new in recovery, it is distressing that on any given day it seems impossible for us to live without regretful actions, thoughtless words, stealing, lying, committing lust in our minds, and slandering others. Yet, it is our failures that show us how desperately we need Jesus. We are beginning to acknowledge that we must come to believe that God *is*, and God *can* if we are to survive, as we are driven to pursue a new and greater relationship with Him.

Our first step in coming to believe is the realization that God through Christ has forgiven us. Today we stand before God as a new person, we are washed clean because He loves us so!

God, thank You for giving me this new life. I need You, God, to help me hear You and to calm the storms of my own thinking. Let me feel Your heartbeat as You pave the way toward freedom. Without You, I will surely fail.

Day 4: *Secure in His Presence*

"I can do all this through him who gives me strength. The grace of the Lord Jesus Christ be with your spirit." Philippians 4:13, 23.

As we proceed through Step Two, we are in the process of coming to believe that God's strength has the power to change our lives in a miraculous way. For so long we have powered through life like a runaway train, bent on getting what we wanted and needed, not caring who we ran over. We cheated, stole from others, and pursued our own desires, which resulted in our paying the supreme sacrifice as we alienated the most important people in our lives.   Reviewing our lives so we don't continue to do the same things over and over again, we acknowledge that Jesus is the source of all life. We realize we must draw near and allow His Spirit to become the breath we take in and exhale out as we begin life authentically—the one He has created just for us.

God's Word promises us we can do all things through Him who gives us strength, and His Word is true whether we are experiencing withdrawal, loss, death, emotional pain, or the boring monotony of life. God can and will strengthen us with the blood of Christ poured out for us on the cross so we can live and do so abundantly for He enriches us with His love. We are coming to believe that He can and will see us through the painful circumstances of life. Day by day we are allowing Him to take up residence in our lives. While some people come alive and aware of God in an instant, our experience is that the process of growing in faith takes time.

While we may struggle, whine, and complain, God continues on about the business of changing us from the inside out. Toddling toward Him with every scrap of trust we can muster, we long for Him to change and bless us. God is a loving, active, and patient Father who cares deeply for us and understands it may take us some time to learn that we can fully trust that His love is real.

He loves us higher, deeper, and wider than we can ever know and as we begin our trust-walk toward Him, we begin to believe that maybe we can do all things through Christ who strengthens us!

God, today let me be alive in Your Spirit, so I can see you in all circumstances. The things of this life cannot prevent You from working in my life; for no other force is greater than You. Calm the racing thoughts in my head and help me see the traps and snares of the evil one. I long to find rest, secured in Your loving presence.

✝

Day 5: *Ten Thousand Thoughts of You*

*"It was through what his Son did that God cleared a path for
everything to come to him — all things in heaven and on earth — for
Christ's death on the cross has made peace with God for all by his
blood. This includes you who were once so far away from God. You
were his enemies and hated him and were separated from him by your
evil thoughts and actions, yet now he has brought you back as his
friends."* Colossians 1:20–21.
(The Living Bible)

Throughout our drinking and using careers and repeatedly
and endlessly falling on our faces, it was impossible to recognize
anything good about ourselves. We spent countless hours, days,
weeks, months, and years planning the next riptide of use or
experiencing the incomprehensible remorse from our last.

Our lives took us far from the will of God; yet with the
painful fallout from our addiction we were driven to our knees
in search of help. We asked for relief and often bargained, "God,
if you keep me out of prison (return my children, keep my job,
help me lose weight, let me win the lotto), I will go to church
every Sunday, stop using drugs or alcohol, gambling, or eating
bad food." Somehow we became convinced that if God would
only deliver us from our rebellion, unmanageability and failure
and give us what we wanted, our lives would be so much better.

Thinking we can "have our cake and eat it too" is nothing
short of immature fantastical thinking; however, recovery
requires that we set aside childish things and put on our big-
person pants. We are about growing up and learning to lean into
God.

87

Despite our current struggle, rebellion has left us vulnerable to addiction. But even so, God has a plan for our lives and His mercies and friendship are new every morning as He longs to spend time with us. Oh, how Jesus loves us!

He lovingly brought us back from complete defeat and presents us as holy and blameless before God and fully equips us with His Spirit. We are wrapped up in the sacrifice of Jesus and presented innocent, pure, and lovely in God's sight. No longer are we condemned for what we have done or continue to do.

Jesus won the battle between our flesh and the evil that whispers in our ears the accusations that threaten to erode our newfound confidence. Bold in our recovery, we stand with Christ in victory against the evil of this world and reject the thoughts of our past failures. Because Christ is for us, no weapon taken up against us will travel through His mighty shield of faith (Ephesians 6:16). Today, we are free and need not fear, for with every step we take, the Holy Spirit is with us to lead, protect, and urge us on to live one more day clean, sober, and in recovery.

God, today let my thoughts be on all You have done for me and not on all the wrong I have committed. When I hyper-focus on my thoughts, motives, and actions while in active addiction, I am rejecting the grace borne out by Your death on the cross. Lord, help my thoughts be on You today. Every time a negative thought of sin and failure comes into my mind, let ten thousand thoughts of You wash it away.

✞

88

Day 6: *Hearing the Shepherd's Voice*

"For you were like sheep going astray, but now you have returned to the Shepherd and Overseer of your souls." 1 Peter 2:25.

The Bible repeatedly uses sheep to portray the failures of the human spirit and our likelihood to wander in search of greener grass or go astray. Although once thought to be one of the dumbest animals, current science has made some interesting discoveries. Sheep are highly intelligent and have the ability to remember other members of their flock, what foods to eat when they are pregnant, and when another sheep is missing. Plus, they are able to shift their attention or focus and recognize faces that are familiar to them.

They are able to differentiate the call of their shepherd from other voices as they are led to feed or the safety of their pasture. Those of us who grew up in organized religion may have heard from the pulpit that God used sheep to portray out stupidity. God, the creator of all things, knows firsthand that the opposite is true. He also knows that we act stupidly when we don't use our God-given resources!

When God uses sheep as an example, it isn't in a derogatory manner because sheep are stupid, but because we are similar to sheep for they are gentle and attuned to the call of their shepherd and capable of trusting him in all things. However, sheep are also likely to follow their own instincts in search of the luscious blades of grass and wander off from the rest of the flock.

And like us, sheep cannot predict the consequences that may follow their wandering (for us it's called rebellion) and need the shepherd to ward off the dangers of predators that lie in wait. Like the wayward sheep, our eyes become fixed on luscious food, winning the lotto, or chasing the feeling of our first high. We seem incapable of surrendering ourselves to the God who wants to love us and give us a safe and beautiful soul-filled life.

As we pursue filling the bottomless pits of our desires, needs, and wants, the cravings for more sex, drugs, gambling, food, or fame, we tumble back into insanity. The consequences remind us that when we follow our own lead and give ourselves over to our desires, we are made sick into our souls as sin envelops our lives. We call this the cycle of despair.

However, this is not the end for us because we realize that our Good Shepherd is there to guide and bring us back into the safety of His presence. No matter what we have done, He walks toward us with concern etched on His face, and with love He reaches out to us and exclaims with relief and happiness that we heard His call.

God, thank You for pursuing me when I go astray and always being there to welcome me home despite what I have done. Thank You for Your goodness despite my self-centered actions. Help me follow Your lead today and not step out in front of Your will for my life. I will follow You as You lead me onto Your path of righteousness.

Day 7: *Half Measures are Deadly*

"Bless the Lord who is my immovable Rock. He gives me strength and skill in battle. He is always kind and loving to me; he is my fortress, my tower of strength and safety, my deliverer. He stands before me as a shield. He subdues my people under me." Psalm 144:1–2
(The Living Bible)

Here's some great advice: "Train your heart to focus on Him and not only your circumstances; believe in His ability and faithfulness. Trust Him when the odds seem stacked against you. Be willing to wait for His timing."[10]

Early recovery is the war between two forces that are alive within us and fighting for dominance. One wants to destroy us and the other desires more than anything else to make us well. Addiction and recovery wage war within us, and even though we may feed our recovery more than our addiction by going to meetings, obtaining a sponsor, and working the steps, we need more.

As we heal and call out to God, the more desperate Satan becomes to bring us back into the devastation of our addictions. We are soldiers on the battlefield and need a general appointed for the express purpose of training us. Soldiers begin their training in boot camp and undergo rigorous training; they are stretched physically and mentally beyond what they at times think they can endure. This training is imperative because soldiers must be prepared to anticipate the battles they may confront and overcome the enemy.

---

[10] Charles Stanley, *Landmines in the Path of the Believer: Avoiding the Hidden Dangers*, (Thomas Nelson, 2008). Pgs. 74–75.

Their hope is to stay alive, so they must learn how to take orders and direction from their commanding officers. Committed soldiers do not train to merely survive the battle but to overcome and defeat their foe, and they are willing to lay down their lives for their fellow soldiers.

Like soldiers, our recovery requires effort and commitment as we strive to overcome the powerful addiction that constantly nags and chirps in our ears. We have learned that applying half measures is deadly. Pursing recovery requires a single-minded, full-measured commitment that includes studying how our addiction works, plots, and plans as the battle lines are drawn.

The odds are stacked against us and it's like we are a battalion of 100 facing an army of 100,000. If we are to survive, we must be committed and diligent and train our hearts to focus on the One who is faithful and will deliver us from all of the painful and overwhelming battles we will face. Racing thoughts, anxiety, withdrawal from substances, broken relationships, lost jobs, poverty, and broken hearts are the result when we enact our own battle plans.

Yet, despite the fact that we continue to take control of things, God still shows up and forgives us our human failures and staunchly defends us because He is faithful. He continues to train us up in Him so the enemy will gain no ground. For we are standing on holy ground and our God is mighty, righteous, and powerful.

God, today let my thoughts be on You. God, let all malice, anger, and all evil thoughts existing within me be silenced. Help me train today for the battles yet to come and prosper in spite of them. I believe You are faithful. Help me rest in the truth of Your faithfulness and be patient, living one day at a time.

Day 8: *Learning to be Patient*

"Answer me when I call to you, my righteous God. Give me relief from my distress; have mercy on me and hear my prayer." Psalm 4:1.

In the midst of our suffering, God is merciful and hears our bitter cries as we call out to Him for help. Sometimes it feels like our desperate prayers are words that leave our mouths and vaporize into thin air.

When we don't see immediate results, fear tells us God isn't listening. Our lives have been so caught up in immediate results so if we can't see it, taste it, and feel it when we think we should, we are convinced this God-thing just isn't working!

We don't realize, though, that He is always working in ways we cannot see. It feels like the words we utter fall into a gigantic hole between our constant suffering and God's existence. Despite our struggle to believe, God really does hear us. It is important that we go through the motions and pray before bed and when we arise in the morning.

We are just now coming to believe and may continue to experience the doubt that He will listen, understand, and respond to our prayers. God is a faithful and righteous God, and we can't hear that enough. He hears our every call and in times of our distress, listens to us as the Spirit whispers for us to hold on and stay the course of our recovery.

Step Two is a time where we must learn to be patient and wait for God to act in His perfect timing. We groan when we hear the word patience, because we are used to substances giving us instantaneous results, and we ache for our suffering to be relieved, the compulsive thoughts about drugs to abate,

93

relationships to be healed, and to be able to financially support ourselves.

Along the way, we begin to see small answers to our prayers and are encouraged as we begin to think that He just might hear us as we offer our weaknesses to Him in prayer. When we look at others who have gone before us and achieved and maintained recovery, we see miracles only God could perform.

When we shift our sight from our own unmet needs and wants and look to the everyday miracles around us, we begin to believe that God is powerful enough to restore street junkies to dedicated and honorable fathers, husbands, and businessmen and prostitutes to loving devoted mothers and wives who seek to honor the Lord.

God doesn't answer in our time, nor does He always answer the way we want, but He always answers according to His will for our lives and those we love. Our prayers are lifted up as we call to God and ask Him to emerge from the shadow of our problems. God is faithful and will relieve us of our suffering and restore peace and balance to our lives.

Thank You, God, for hearing me in my time of distress. Help me believe, God, when I doubt You love me and want to help me. God I've spent so many years at a distance from Your goodness and holiness. Let me see You in the glory of You and bask in the love You have for me. God, help me see You in the power of the cross and the salvation You have so freely given.

✝

Day 9: *The Rock of Our Recovery*

"The Lord is my rock, my fortress and deliverer; my God is my rock, in whom I take refuge, my shield and the horn of my salvation, my stronghold. I called to the Lord, who is worthy of praise, and I have been saved from my enemies." Psalm 18:2–3.

Addiction is not our friend. It is a liar and deceiver. It is a force that has thrown us here and there and watched in silent glee as our bodies and spirits were beaten. Addiction ravaged our minds and twisted and warped our thinking. It sought to saturate our minds with its lies, and insatiable appetites.

Recovery isn't easy, and we realize we have been granted a daily reprieve from the obsessive thoughts of our addiction. Step Two encourages us to accept that God is our only defense over this evil that wants to consume and destroy us. We run toward God for He is our rock and cannot be moved; no power nor principality can destroy or overcome Him as He wages war against the powers of darkness that are trying to eradicate the good that God is doing in our lives.

But God builds a structure of hope all around us that the enemy cannot break through, for our God's protection is mighty and impenetrable. This world is full of trouble, and we have had our share. However, we have learned that we can call on God and take our refuge in Him when we feel defeated or overwhelmed. Our surrender is the foundation to accept His grace in Step Three. God's presence in our lives is showing us that we are safe and secure as we live with Him in each moment of every day.

How comforting it is to have the One True God as our stronghold in times of intense battle! The war rages on between recovery and active addiction. And even though we will have troubles, and even though Satan fights to keep us oppressed with all his might and evil tactics of warfare, the battle for our soul is over because we have come to believe that Jesus Christ is our salvation.

We believe He came, He died, and He rose again so we might have life, and the Spirit of Christ is alive within our hearts. The plague of addiction is a destructive force and the recovery skills gifted to us are the path to our wholeness as we learn to walk with God. God has given us His weapons of war, and His sacrifice has provided the shield, the horn, and stronghold of our faith.

We take refuge in our faith even though at times we are knocked down, overcome, and seemingly defeated; however, we train our eyes on Him, not our pain, as we rely on Him for the strength we need to overcome the difficulties in this life. He is our deliver, our defender, and our strength who frees us from our war-torn existence.

God, today help me keep my eyes on the prize. God, deliver me from the enemy. You are the rock of my recovery and I cannot be moved from this way of life. Be my shield in times of intense battle, protecting my heart and mind. Be my deliverer as my eyes remain steadfast on You.

✞

Day 10: *The Catalyst of Suffering*

"For truly I tell you, many prophets and righteous people longed to see what you see but did not see it, and to hear what you hear but did not hear it." Matthew 13:17.

It rubs raw against our warped understanding of God to think the craziness of our active addiction has opened our ears to actually hear and begin listening to God. We have only to look at our dented car, low-rent apartments, and minimum wage jobs as the evidence of our years or decades of doing things our own way.

Thousands of self-centered needs, wants, and desires have tumbled our lives into a shamble, and we see ourselves as the lowest form of humankind. We wonder how God can love us for we can barely stand to be in the same room with ourselves! Failure is all around us even at the grocery store as we see a mother with her child and are reminded that our own child was taken from us by child protection services and is even now in a foster home or permanently adopted by someone else.

The trauma of loss is triggered, and we wonder what would be the point of knowing a God who let this happen to us and our children? Whatever our personal tragedy, our history with religion, or the wrongs we have committed in the past, Jesus is waiting to come in and heal our hurts.

We may think it is impossible, but He wants to love and comfort us to our very core. Even though we have not lived perfect lives, we have heard His call and felt His presence as He has come in so we could taste and see that God is good.

Maybe in the eyes of society we are losers, but in the eyes of our God we are righteous, and we respond by training our eyes on His loving face. As people in recovery, we have been delivered from hopelessness. We have experienced firsthand being delivered from a disease that Satan tried to use to destroy us and hurt our children, families, and loved ones in one fell swoop.

But Jesus chose to lay down His life for us and reaches out to us—addicts and alcoholics who are often living the most lowly and despicable of lives in our society, a ragtag group of people from all walks of life—in friendship and healing. Oh, what a friend we have in Jesus!

God, today let me rejoice in my suffering because it has allowed me to see and hear You. Let my suffering be the catalyst to hear You better and see You more clearly. God, You know my needs even before I do. Today I place my hope and confidence in You.

Day 11: *The Constancy of God*

"But he gives us more and more strength to stand against all such
evil longings. As the Scripture says, God gives strength to the humble
but sets himself against the proud and haughty. So, give yourselves
humbly to God. Resist the devil and he will flee from you."
James 4:6–7.
(The Living Bible)
Suggested Reading: *Twelve Steps and Twelve Traditions*, pg. 31.

Prayers sent and unanswered, children lost despite
continual and earnest prayer tempt us to hold God accountable
for our failures. Maybe we've never been the praying sort of
person, yet we think we are entitled to have God do what we
think is right!

In addiction we were driven by our desires and wants and
stubbornly believed our mission was to control things—
everything. It never dawned on us that we were standing in
opposition to God's will and His perfect design for our lives. For
sure, every now and then we cast a thought in God's direction
and once in a great while—and usually when we were in
trouble—we were driven to talk to Him and ask Him "why?"
Despite the fact we are in recovery, we still tend to have mono-
vision and only see the prayers that haven't been answered and
dwell on the awful things in life where we think God should
have done something.

In our cloud of self-obsession, we are unaware (and
unaware that we are unaware) that God has answered countless
unspoken prayers and kept our child safe from a sex offender or
prevented our car from swerving into a bus full of children as

we drove drunk. Right now, He may be answering a thousand other things to prevent further harm to us.

Recovery is a new way for us to live, and what we pray for in earnest today may bring more pain to our lives. God holds all knowledge of what is good and what is damaging to us.

We are coming to believe that the power of God relieves us from the sting of defeat that obsession and compulsion leave at our door. We are told that recovery requires us to make an extreme sacrifice so that we might live. We have only to look to the cross to understand what that really means. When life hurts because our families turn away from us, or our children — even when raised in recovery for multiple years — reject us, we are tempted to blame God.

But, praying in earnest, we long for and know that God hears us. When He doesn't answer, we are tempted to be angry and then may feel guilty for our feelings. However, we are just learning who God is and He can handle our hurts, disappointments, and anger.

God is constant. His arms are wide open, ready to embrace and heal our broken hearts. God is good, loving, and cares for us as we move toward Him. and the perfect plan He offers.

God, today let my faith and confidence be in You, not myself, and not in all the things I see, think or feel, or in my own wisdom. Let my focus be on You and may patience and perseverance be the gifts You have for me today. I am not used to waiting for things, God, and the pain inside me is so great. God, right now I bring to You all of my hurts like a little child with broken toys. Even now God, You are making all things new.

✟

Day 12: *Inviting God into Our Lives*

"Set me free from my prison, that I may praise your name."
Psalm 142:7.

It is easy to recall the hundreds if not thousands of times we prayed and bartered with God to relieve us of addiction's painful consequences. These times of suffering have brought us face to face with the powerlessness of repeating the same behavior over and over again that lead us to reenact defeating behaviors and re-experience pain.

Still holding grudges against God for not protecting us from these sickening, horrible, and dreadful consequences of addiction and damning ourselves for being vile human beings, we hear people in the rooms tell us easy does it! Recovery is a process that restores our lives to a sane way of living, so it is really important that we resist judging ourselves harshly and think God is doing the same thing.

There is time enough for us to inventory the circumstances of our lives and how addiction has left the ugly scars no one can see. It is important to understand that God is patient and kind and is in control of all the circumstances that shoot shards of pain through our hearts.

Slowly and deliberately we are being brought into His presence as we seek freedom from the sin, pain, and the consequences of this fallen world. Thinking we had found our hope and happiness in drugs, food, shopping or man's mystical philosophies, the luster has worn off and we have come face to face with the fact that addiction is a prison that holds us captive to its demands.

Giving thanks to God, we are willing to commit ourselves to a way of living where we give our whole heart to God. We are falling face-first into His will, and instead of living double lives with drunkenness, gluttony, sexual sin, anger, pride and resentment, we are now committed to pursuing God. As we learn to depend on God, we throw ourselves heart first into this process. Recovery calls us to action, and we are beginning to believe God knows best.

We are learning what it means to let go. In gratitude we acknowledge the humble beginnings of our journey toward Christ and the tiny mustard seed of faith that perhaps He can and will help us.

God, help me hear You today. You hold the key to unlock the door leading to freedom from this prison of wasted thoughts, feelings and self-defeating emotions. As I cast my cares on You and bring all the overwhelming circumstances of life to the foot of the cross, I invite You into my life to guide me and show me the way You would have me go.

Day 13: *Believing Through Our Doubts*

"Jesus said, 'If? There are no "ifs" among believers. Anything can happen.' No sooner were the words out of his mouth than the father cried, 'Then I believe. Help me with my doubts!'" Mark 9:23-24
(The Message)
Suggested Reading: *Alcoholics Anonymous Big Book*, pg. 47[11].

After spending long and lonely periods of time standing on the fringes of society, we're amazed that we're beginning to experience who God is, what He likes and dislikes, how He loves, and who He loves. Overwhelming as it may be, God has been trying to get our attention so we can learn how good He is and so He can give us the great life that awaits us.

Through our poor choices and maladaptive ways of getting our wants, needs, and desires met, our beliefs about God's power has become twisted and warped. We have blamed our disappointment on everything but our use of substances. Our relationship with God has become out of sync with the truth of who He is and who we are and how much we need Him.

We have fallen prey to the deceiving and destructive nature of our addiction. Some of us never thought it important to believe in God or even acknowledge that there is one, because we had done just fine on our own. Yet, here we are feeling absolutely miserable! It is easier, we think, to believe in cause and effect — or karma as some of us call it — and think all this God talk is a bunch of mumbo jumbo. After all, God is only for weak and foolish people.

Perhaps we believe there is a source of higher power, and on a good day we really have no use for it: On a bad day we

---

[11] *Alcoholics Anonymous Big Book*, (The Anonymous Press; 2008).

wonder why it has allowed these things to happen to us? Whatever our history may be, we are now open and ready to learn more about this God who is ready to help prepare us for the life we want more than anything else.

Ready to learn about God, we begin to read about the reality of how much He loves us and patiently waits for us to turn to Him. It is normal, at this time in our recovery, to think that our actions can control how God moves in our lives.

We may think that if we pray in the right way by throwing ourselves face-first on the floor for just the right amount of time, God will be pleased and will do what we want. But, we are learning that we cannot control God, yet we can please Him and become willing to believe that maybe—just maybe—He really does care for us! Before now, even if we knew there was a God, we had no idea what it was like to experience unconditional love and acceptance or walk with Him hand in hand and heart to heart.

Today, we will rest in the confidence that in this moment nothing else matters as we come to believe that He loves us and wants our very best. Just Him, just us, for we believe.

God, today I will take Your hand of friendship and love since You are the author of my life and the one who makes perfect my faith. Let me walk and grow as You guide me, hand in hand on the path of recovery. I believe in you, God. Thank You, Jesus, for covering me in Your righteousness and for Your sacrifice so that I can enjoy fellowship with the Father.

☦

Day 14: *Fuzzy Bears and Heart Shaped Candy*

"Love is very patient and kind, never jealous or envious, never boastful or proud, never haughty or selfish or rude. Love does not demand its own way. It is not irritable or touchy. It does not hold grudges and will hardly even notice when others do it wrong. It is never glad about injustice but rejoices whenever truth wins out." 1 Corinthians 13:4-6.
(The Living Bible)

February 14th is one of the loneliest days in Western culture. "It's Valentine's Day!" and groans can be heard all across the country. It's the day of love! Flowers, jewelry, and candy fly off the shelves as billions of dollars are spent on the perfect gift so we can show our loved one how much we care.

Even before Christmas is over, you can see the red heart-shaped candy boxes lining the shelves of stores and teddy bears holding engagement rings in the jewelry store display case. However romantic, this day can be a painful time for us lonely hearts. Alone and dejected, we wonder if God will ever bring the right person into our lives. *Hallmark* movies with perfect people finding love make us wonder what is wrong with us! Why can't we be the beneficiary of this romantic reality everyone else seems to have?

Our hearts are heavy, and we feel the pangs of loneliness that cut so deep that sometimes we even miss our abuser. Everywhere we look, people are holding hands, sharing a meal, and seem to have everything we have ever wanted but have so far been denied. Valentine's Day can be fun and a wonderful time to express how much we love someone, yet it can also be a distraction from the source of the only love that can truly satisfy and last for all eternity.

Instead of focusing on what we don't have, it is important that we focus on what we *do* have, for God loves us exactly as we are right now. He loves us despite our flaws and dishonesty, and even though we are self-seeking, fearful, and faithless, we can trust and have confidence in how wide and deep His love is for us.

The world all around us is fallen, and it makes sense that sin has twisted the true meaning of love. Heart-shaped balloons, red roses, boxes of chocolates and fuzzy bears don't cause our hearts to swell or beat with excitement! Instead our hearts contract with pain because they are still bruised from the loss of our children, family members, or spouses due to addiction's mighty sting.

But the good news is that despite our losses, God is showing us what true love is! His love is patient, kind, rejoices in the truth, protects, perseveres, and never fails. We can place our hope in His love. We can be assured that God is working in our lives as He transforms us into a new creation.

Today we are holy and blameless because we find our hope in Him. As we turn to Him and ask Him to heal our hearts, we have just taken the first step of faith as we come to believe God can restore our lives and that soon, He will turn our pain into joy and set our feet to dancing.

God, today I will rejoice in the love You have for me. Even when I am stuck in my own suffering, You are patient and kind and will never fail. Even when things don't go as I have planned, You are in control. And in my love for You, God, I will trust in You.

✞

Day 15: *The God Spot*

"Submit yourselves, then, to God. Resist the devil, and he will flee from you. Come near to God and he will come near to you."
James 4:7–8.
Suggested Reading: *Alcoholics Anonymous Big Book*, pg. 57

It seems as though once we are sober and stop hurting ourselves, life starts to level out. We begin to experience the reprieve and balance between pain and comfort, despair and relief. During these times of reprieve and balance, we may begin to sense It seems as though once we are sober and stop hurting ourselves, life starts to level out. We begin to experience the reprieve and balance between pain and comfort, despair and relief. During these times of reprieve and balance, we may begin to sense an emerging need for something different than we could ever find in drugs, alcohol, shopping, gambling, food, sex, or any other substance we used to escape reality. It is here, buried deep inside of us, where our "God spot" exists, and it is indistinguishable from the beating of our hearts.

It is a place that longs to break free from the chaos of self. It is a place that desires the Spirit of Christ, the Spirit of something beautiful, good, lovely, and comforting. It is the place we intuitively know is there. Sometimes we feel and recognize it during or after a torrent of tears when the pain of loss becomes so great we feel we can no longer go on.

It is a place so fragile and underdeveloped that often we can't see it or articulate what it is because it is hidden — encased and surrounded by layers of regret and grief for all that has come and gone.

Recovery is a blessing, and when we surrender and submit ourselves to God, we touch this beautiful and awe-inspiring place about which poets write beautiful sonnets. It is a place easily confused with romantic love, and it drives us powerfully to do things we might never otherwise do. As human beings, we look to the temporal things of this world to fill our God spot.

Full of delusion, we justify our self-centered behaviors and end up more lonely and less self-fulfilled that we were to begin with. Step Two readies us to surrender our personal philosophies and manmade recipes for success and to ready ourselves to receive God as He unfolds His love, comfort, knowledge, wisdom, and truth.

After unsuccessfully trying to find just the right job, relationship, car, child, or spouse to make us feel worthy, loved, and whole, it isn't until God takes hold of our hearts that we realize only He can fill the void inside us. When Jesus comes in, Satan has no choice but to flee! Our recovery sends him scurrying away as God emerges victorious!

God, today I want to allow You into my life to guide and show me Your ways. Let me acknowledge your wisdom and power, Father. Sometimes I hurt so much and long for You. I long to go home. Let me instead be of use to You today. As I look to You, help me do what You would have me do. Help me be useful to You and my fellow man.

✝

Day 16: *As Peace Settles In*

"So, look upon your old sin nature as dead and unresponsive to sin, and instead be alive to God, alert to him, through Jesus Christ our Lord. Do not let sin control your puny body any longer; do not give in to its sinful desires." Romans 6:11–12.

In Step One we acknowledged that we were powerless over our addiction and began to realize that some source of power had to take control of our lives because we had lost it! Looking all around us, we saw the wreckage of our addiction.

No longer doubting we are a people who have been brought from death to life, we are grateful God has delivered us from the mayhem of insanity our disease has created. It seems like forever since we felt this sane and we're surprised at this feeling of peace settling in over our lives. What an amazing gift God has given us: because Jesus died for our sins, we are no longer unprotected or powerless.

He has brought God's own power to our lives! We have the power of the God of the heavens and earth — the same God who spoke the universe into motion and scooped dirt up from the earth, fashioned it into His own image, and breathed life into its nostrils!

Recovery is a lifelong process and we are learning about who this God is and are beginning to believe He can deliver us from the powerful urges, thoughts, and desires that have brought such pain into our lives. We unapologetically acknowledge that without God, the power of our addiction will bring nothing but spiritual and physical destruction.

We are convinced that no other power can relieve us from the peril we face. Recovery presents us with the choice of life or death. Having traveled this bitter road long enough and trying everything we thought would relieve us of our obsession, we are left with no choice but to acknowledge with each breath we take that God must be everything.

There are those who will say it is only the weak who surrender their personal power to God, but we know the opposite is true. Weakness makes us stronger, and we know that God is well pleased, on our side, and cheers us on in our process of coming to believe we must surrender to Him!

Our understanding of God is deepening as He delivers us from death and shows us the way to everlasting life. Offering ourselves to God, holy and blameless in Jesus, we begin to realize how God is changing us, one day, one obsessive thought, and one compulsive action at a time. Today we offer ourselves to God as He breathes new life into our hearts.

God, today I ask You to show me new ways to turn from sin, as I long to hear You louder than my own destructive thoughts. God, may knowing You better be my only desire. Be mine today, O God, for I thirst for Your presence in my life.

Day 17: *The Similarities are Undeniable*

"For the wrath of God is revealed from heaven against all ungodliness
and unrighteousness of men, who suppress the truth in
unrighteousness, because what may be known of God is manifest in
them, for God has shown it to them." Romans 1:18-20.
(New King James Version)
Suggested Reading: *Alcoholics Anonymous Big Book,* page 55.

Belonging to the recovery community allows us to see ourselves reflected in others as they disclose how addiction caused their lives to cycle out of control. Just like us, they had to expend extraordinary amounts of energy to deny, run, and hide from addiction. In the end, running served no purpose — addiction had its way.

As people in recovery, we share many things in common, and while we are all from different walks of life, the similarities are undeniable. The most common similarity is that on our own, we could not stop the destruction of addiction and needed help from each other and a power greater than ourselves.

It can be overwhelming when we begin to accept the truth that we need God. No clearer picture do we need than when we look at how we used places, people, and things to feed and justify our addiction.

Step Two enables us to see how God has poked and prodded us along the rocky road of recovery. While it's not hard for us to identify the difficulties addiction had created, our thick-headed delusional thinking blinds us to the fact that God loves us and has been with us during the worst of times. Shame clogs our ears from hearing the loving and subtle voice of our Father calling out as He tells us He loves us and wants our very best.

We find it difficult to believe that God was with us when we stole, cheated, and cursed His name. We struggle with believing there is anything God could possibly find about us that is good.

The why there is Jesus: Jesus poured His life out on the cross and made it possible for God to claim us. His blood washed away our sin and lit the cathedrals of our hearts simply because He had great compassion and love for us.

Many of us have clung to the idea of a God on high, far apart and separate from us. But God is real and unchanging and longs to show us just how much He cares for us. He waits patiently for us to realize that we need His power so that He can fill the empty cavern in the middle of our chest. He waits for us to acknowledge that we need a friend and an advocate with the authority and power to direct our lives and fill us with His Spirit.

We are convinced beyond any doubt that filling ourselves with extemporaneous things doesn't work, because we have tried countless unsuccessful ways to change ourselves. We've tried to boost our image, change jobs or lovers, stuff ourselves with food, and use drugs, alcohol, and music all to no avail because nothing has ever filled the ache of deep longing. It is when the things of this world fall away that we realize only God can make us whole and fill our hearts. He is waiting for us to invite Him in as He continues to call to the deep places in our hearts.

God clear away the things of this world so I can hear You, see You and taste of the good things You have for me. God, be my friend. I want to walk with You, talk with You, and experience the truth of Your fellowship today.

Day 18: *Watched Over by God's Angels*

"If you say, 'The Lord is my refuge,' and you make the Most High your dwelling, no harm will overtake you, no disaster will come near your tent. For he will command his angels concerning you to guard you in all your ways." Psalm 91:9–11.

The first place we turn when life gets tough and things aren't going our way is to the things that the world has to offer. Good or indifferent, we are tempted to look to pop-psychology, the worldly advice of Dr. Phil, drugs, sex, entertainment, sports, a new car, entertainment idols, or other pleasures to fill us up when life gets difficult.

Even as we begin to experience trust in God, we are taken by surprise when our grip holding fast to God slips and we find ourselves insecure and full of fear. Anger fills us with rage, and we can't figure out exactly why this is all happening to us again. Perhaps we are in trouble at work, our spouse is nagging at us, the kids are a mess, and we don't have enough money to pay our rent.

Sometimes life just happens, and at other times when we take a step back, we can see where we stepped out ahead of God and thought we had this recovery thing in the bag. Our slippery slope began with a little sin here and a self-centered indulgence there, and we rationalized we have been doing so well in our recovery that we deserved a reward. Before long, we see how denial, rationalization, and minimization are in full swing paving the way for disaster.

It is almost a relief when our ideas of what we think will make us happy come crashing down and we are driven to our knees in sweet relief that we need God to guide us. We need

Jesus day to day — and moment to moment — or we are doomed to do the same thing over and over again, producing the same results of unhappiness, sorrow, and pain.

Instant forgetters and all, we need God to dwell in our hearts to nurture, strengthen, and build a resolve within us to remain committed to our recovery. It is a lifelong process and at times we find ourselves struggling with self-will. But we have the assurance that God, regardless of what we do, commands His angels over us.

He is concerned for our welfare and guards us in all of His excellent ways. Even though at times it may not feel like it, we are not alone as we grapple with our hurts, pains, and defects of character. We have come to believe that He will strengthen and guide us and has commanded His angels concerning our welfare in the event we lose our way. Our God is good, faithful, holy and true.

God, today knowing You are there to guide me, I will walk in Your ways and by Your truth. How treasured I am that You command the angels to guard and keep watch over me. I am safe in Your keeping. Thank You, God, for loving me. You are so good!

Day 19: *Long, Wide, Deep, and High Love*

> *"And I pray that Christ will be more and more at home in your
> hearts, living within you as you trust in him. May your roots go
> down deep into the soil of God's marvelous love; and may you be able
> to feel and understand, as all God's children should, how long, how
> wide, how deep, and how high his love really is; and to experience this
> love for yourselves, though it is so great that you will never see the
> end of it or fully know or understand it. And so at last you will be
> filled up with God himself." Ephesians 3:17–19.*
> *(The Living Bible)*
> *"Let go of impoverished, circumscribed,*
> *and finite perceptions of God."*[12]

Working Step Two may mean that we have started
attending church as we seek out this source of power called God;
we are trying to find out where He lives and exactly what it is
He wants from us if we are to stay clean and sober. We listen in
meetings and in places of worship, and the words that flow from
the mouths of men tell us that God loves us. This thought is so
foreign to us because up until this point, our perception of God
has been distant, or it has been up-close and devastatingly
painful.

Whatever our experience, it is almost impossible not to
project onto God a limited concept based on our sorrows. Stuck
in the warped perceptions of what His love looks and feels like,
we stand in the midst of our blurred perception of who He must
be.

While we long to experience the truth of who God is and
feel Him in our hearts, our brokenness tends to limit our ability

---

[12] Manning, *Ragamuffin Gospel*, p. 202.

to experience Him. We think, "This can't work," as we recall the God-in-the-box who we are convinced is void of compassion, care, and love for us. This negative perception is based on our limited knowledge of Him and our extensive experience with failure—and, OH, how we long to be rid of it!

But the good news is that when we are willing to cultivate a new relationship and brush off our old ways of thinking. No longer are we held captive by our faulty and unhealthy thoughts of who God is. As we open ourselves and become willing to meet God in a new relationship, we discover that the false god we experienced in active addiction was a small god that was powered by self and uninterested in our well-being.

In fact, that perception drove us further into the darkness of our addiction. Coming to believe that our hope is found in Jesus—who wants a new relationship with us—we break through and accept the fact that in order to live, we need a God who is greater, more powerful, and infinitely more loving than the small and false god of our old life.

We are convinced that we need an all-powerful and down-deep-in-our-souls God who loves us with an unquenchable fire and who wants to have an intimate and lifelong relationship with us.

God, today open my eyes to the depth and power of love for me through Jesus Christ. Let me walk in Your ways and see You in all things. God, forgive me for my limited experience and perception of Your greatness. You are the one true God—all-powerful, holy, and loving.

✢

Day 20: *Letting God's Glory Fall*

"Come to me and I will give you rest – all of you who work so hard beneath a heavy yoke. Wear my yoke – for it fits perfectly – and let me teach you; for I am gentle and humble, and you shall find rest for your souls; for I give you only light burdens." Matthew 11:28.
(The Living Bible)
Suggested Reading: Alcoholics Anonymous Big Book, pages 46–47.

As we gaze at the cross where Jesus sacrificed His all so that we might have life, we need to get ready for the glory of God to fall hard all around us. God's compassion for us is extraordinary. He desires every person from every corner of the earth to seek Him, know Him, and enter into a deep and abiding relationship that will last for eternity.

God is pleased, honored, and blessed when we earnestly seek Him. He is there in every moment, with every wisp of time just waiting for us to turn our eyes toward Him and accept all that He has to offer. God's love is broad; it is deep; it is wide; and it does not discriminate.   He loves all, is in all, and desires all. When we put our hope, our faith in Jesus Christ, the One who gave it all so we might have the gift of intimate fellowship with God, we have made our decision to live again. It is as if we have awoken for the first time and realized our own thoughts had given God a bad reputation as an aloof and angry God who doesn't work for any good in our lives.

When we acknowledge what a wonderful work God has already done in us through our recovery, we find peace and gratitude. Moments of ease accompany the freedom we have found, and we experience the willingness to stop trying to control everything and instead wonder what He wants us to do.

117

What a wonderful and glorious thing it is to put our faith and confidence in Jesus and trust in His will for our lives. For most of our lives, we have been unable to trust anyone or any power; however, today we have this beautiful and extraordinary mustard seed of faith that causes our hearts to swell with new hope. These moments of faith fill us with hope, and we want to dance with joy at the hope that overflows into our hearts.

Step Two has given us the opportunity to let God in and open our hearts, our ears so that we can hear the call of His voice. We begin to pray for others and ask God's to help them hear too!

Sometimes we are stunned by this new development, but we feel ready to think about someone other than ourselves. That we uttered a prayer for someone else seems miraculous. The evidence of His presence in our lives is our ability now to hear His call and attend to His will.

God, thank You for loving us, for loving me even in times of sin when I displease you the most. I know even though I sin, the perfection of Christ covers me, and I am holy and blameless in Your sight. What a friend I have in Jesus!

Day 21: *A Dose of Hope*

"Jesus replied, 'What is impossible with man is possible with God.'"
Luke 18:27.

As we searched for ways to fend off the insanity of our addiction, we have consulted with a variety of people. We were desperately looking for ways to be relieved of our painful feelings, losses, and depression that are associated with the consequences of our addiction. Perhaps it was a clergyman, doctor, counselor, psychologist, mentor, parent or other family member we hoped could help us.

We were desperate for help and hoped they could help us feel better *and* yet avoid our need to stop using the substance of our choice. Clawing our way toward some sort of relief, no matter how hard we tried — despite the sound advice received — we were completely unable to beat back the pain for any length of time.

It seemed nothing and no one was able to relieve the sickness in our souls. Yet, there were brief moments of respite when love and acceptance were offered by professionals and spiritual advisors who tried to help us, a small seed of hope that things could be different started to stir. As we experienced these glimmers and moments of hopeful reprieve, they were followed by a huge disappointment when our addiction descended on us again in full force.

The advice and comfort were temporary and unable to produce long-term solutions to our problems. In desperation, we truly tried just about anything to help us and in frustration until we became ready to lay our will down and cry out to God that without Him we can do nothing.

Step Two has whipped up a dose of hopefulness as we are coming to believe that with God, recovery is possible. Without this source of power, we are lost and hopeless and this addiction, alcoholism, or whatever "ism" must be crushed if we are to survive. Standing on the precipice of change, we realize that a wonderful life-changing event has occurred in our hearts. As we put forth effort, faith sprouts up in our hearts and graces us with change and healing. No one has to convince us of the truth that God exists, because we have experienced in a very real way that what was impossible with man is possible with God. Standing in hope, we lean into our new faith because the truth of what Jesus did for us on the cross has come alive in our lives.

We are coming to believe that His words of truth and actionable sacrifice are powerfully at work and alive as they fill our lives with hope. New hope opens our hearts as we press on to experience Him in every moment of every day.

God, today let my words be few and let them fall on me heavy in truth and hope. God, I have tried so many things to change the outcomes in my life. I realize it is in the quiet corners of my existence that You wait patiently for me to surrender so that You can come in. God, let Your strength and might be evident for all to see how great is our God!

Day 22: *Raw and Real Change*

*"You want what you don't have, so you kill to get it. You long for
what others have, and can't afford it, so you start a fight to take it
away from them. And yet the reason you don't have what you want is
that you don't ask God for it. And even when you do ask you don't
get it because your whole aim is wrong — you want only what will
give you pleasure." James 4:2–3.*
(The Living Bible)
Suggested Reading: *Twelve Steps and Twelve Traditions,* page 38.

It's striking how we raised our fists toward God while
shouting or shrieking about the bitter consequences of our
addiction. We may still believe that others have done us wrong
and remain sore and burned up that they didn't deal fairly with
us or give us what we wanted. Begging, pleading and
bemoaning the pain in our hearts, we complained that our loved
ones didn't trust us.

Completely immersed in self-pity, we were incapable of
seeing how this way of thinking chained us to the pain and
trauma of our victimhood and blinded as to how desperately we
needed help. "Dear God," we pleaded, "Please don't let this
happen to me; help me God!" Yet, once the moments of trauma
and pain passed and we received some relief, we closed
ourselves off and refused to listen to the words of advice offered
by those who were witnessing our downward spiral.

After praying and experiencing relief, we promised God we
would change, go to church, stop engaging in sexual sin or going
to bars or the fast-food restaurant, or use credit cards. However
as hope and change were closing in, our "instant forgetters"
were at play and we did an about-face, forgetting what we

promised in our heartfelt prayers to God. Fueled by self-will, off we went once again, striking out on our own and leaving God in the wind.

Time and again, it took being faced with the dire consequences of our addiction to make us willing to look to a higher power to take control and change us. We are not quick studies, and sometimes it isn't until we experience — perhaps for the hundredth time — a thorough butt-kicking that we become willing to change. Thank God that finally we are beginning to ready ourselves to experience "Thy will" in a raw, real, and life-changing way.

Being open, honest, and willing to listen to the counsel of our sponsor, we come to believe God is much more than a wish-granting, Santa-inspired seasonal or situational source of power. Today we are surrounded by the power of the Holy Spirit, and we feel this life-giving source seep deep into our hearts.

God, thank You for letting me experience these times of butt-kicking and character building so that I can live and grow and learn more about who You are. I ask that You continue to refine my experiences — whether they are good or bad — and create a foundation of faith so I can live a life perfectly designed for me by You.

Day 23: *Celebrating His Gift*

"There is no eternal doom awaiting those who trust him to save them. But those who don't trust him have already been tried and condemned for not believing in the only Son of God. Their sentence is based on this fact: that the Light from heaven came into the world, but they loved the darkness more than the Light, for their deeds were evil. They hated the heavenly Light because they wanted to sin in the darkness. They stayed away from that Light for fear their sins would be exposed and they would be punished." John 3:18–20.

No one really wants to get old, yet we live in a world where being young, beautiful, and musically gifted is of high value, and being wrinkly, fat, worn out, old, or down on our luck is to be avoided at all costs. Most of us have the drive to enjoy pleasure, delight, and as we age, start out on the journey to retain our youth.

Our appetites for happiness and fulfillment seem insatiable. We spend billions of dollars per year with music lessons, beauty treatments, new cars, clothes, boats, facials, manicures, pedicures, cosmetics, and cosmetic procedures all to avoid or ward off the passing of time and the many seasons of life. We think becoming irrelevant, elderly, or out of style on the fringes of society should be avoided at all costs!

However, what we long for and spend all our resources on as we look for eternal youth is a mirage; it is an empty promise leading us to a dead end. We will get old (if we are lucky) and each line and wrinkle have a story to tell. But we have something of eternal value that eclipses even the most rare and beautiful jewel because God gave us life instead of death. God is extraordinary and benevolent, and He is holy, holy, holy!

Awestruck angels cry out day and night at the majesty of His presence. This same indescribable God made a way for us to enjoy eternal youth and it costs us nothing! All God asks is that we believe that He loves us and has sent His Son Jesus so He can love us with every ounce of eternity that is His to give. This may be difficult for us to believe, but our recovery demands that we consider and wonder who God is and surrender as we prepare to ask Him to come in and guide us in our recovery.

Being saved or being born again begins with a decision: the decision to believe that God loved us so much He sent His only Son to die and pay the price to ransom *my* soul, cover *my* sins, and heal *my* life, scouring out every sin hidden deep in my heart. The only requirement to receive this gift is the willingness to begin to believe He loves *me* utterly and completely.

Temporary fixes are temporary. But God is the eternal fix as He creates a special place just for us in the afterlife. Today, let us listen to the call of His voice as He whispers His love song to come near and taste and see that He is good, loving, and able to supply all of our needs.

God, today I will celebrate this gift! As I come to believe in Your goodness and the gift of Jesus Christ, who paid it all, let my life be an example of Your radical, transforming, and everlasting gift of life.

Day 24: *Taking God out of the Box*

"So, you see, our love for him comes as a result of his loving us first."
1 John 4:19.
(The Living Bible)

"Human love will always be a faint shadow of God's love. Not because it is too sugary or sentimental but simply because it can never compare from whence it comes. Human love with all its passion and emotion is a thin echo of the passion/emotion love of Yahweh."[13]

Our broken experiences of love have thrust us through the doors of the Twelve-Step program—bruised, worn out, and beat up and bleeding—with an intense longing for something or someone to fill us up. We are empty and crave to feel a part of something so we can experience a special connection with a special someone.

Yet, throughout our lifetime this thing we think is love has always slipped through our fingers or ended with resentment, hurt, bitterness or trauma. As we attend meetings we hear members in the Twelve-Step program share confidently and with smiles on their faces, "Let us love you, until you can love yourself" and "Let the group be a power greater than yourselves until you can come to believe."

While these words might make us want to hurl at first, we need to hear them as words of comfort. We cannot recover all by ourselves or without other people who care enough to answer the phone at 2 in the morning or to come and sit with us while we cry rivers of tears and grieve over all that we have lost.

---

[13] Manning, *Ragamuffin Gospel, p. 100.*

As loving as the actions of our recovery friends are, they cannot compare to the love God offers. Oh, how we cheat ourselves out of the marvelous and wondrous, incomprehensible love of God when we believe the only love available to us is from man! We spend inordinate amounts of time trying to replicate the image of God's love as we write, sing, dance, and whine about wanting it or not having it.

The lyrics and big beat of rap are completely obsessed with how a relationship has gone wrong, or traditional loves songs coo about how a man craves a beautiful woman with eyes like emeralds and hair that shimmers in the sunlight. The prose of perfection and agony of loss can go on forever. Romantic love is beautiful; yet it can be extraordinarily painful when we suffer the sting of rejection.

After a time, we realize that human love — whether in the form of friendship or romantic love — eventually fails because it is not powerful enough to change us where it hurts. Exactly who is God and what does this love He has for us mean or look like? We tend to think about God in our own terms and can't help but put Him in a box and label it with our misperceptions.

Slowly, we are beginning to see that our misperceptions have poisoned the well of all things spiritual after spending most of our lives limiting God's power and grace as we continue to fall for the deceptiveness of the world. Beginning Step Two, we may only be able to see our support group as our higher power as the first step toward surrender. Each of us must at some point take that first step of faith as we walk out on the water and attend to the call of Jesus.

We will stumble and falter, but His voice will grow louder each day as we step forward in the faith that God can and will restore us to sanity. Venturing forward into Step Two, no longer are we willing to limit God's reality or fall prey to the darkness

126

of this world. We are standing on the doorstep of this very real, life-giving and awesome reality of God.

God, today let me step out of the shadow of Your love and into the full sunlight of Your Spirit. Let me see Your love, God, as it exists in every moment and in every breath I take. Let all that I am absorb the love and life You have for me!

Day 25: *Don't Despise Small Beginnings*

"Truly I tell you, if you have faith as small as a mustard seed, you can say to this mountain, 'Move from here to there,' and it will move. Nothing will be impossible for you." Matthew 17:20

Wondering if we will ever have the faith necessary to stay clean and sober, it's important to realize that even the greatest of spiritual giants still only has faith the size of a mustard seed in contrast to the greatness of our God. Mustard seed-sized faith is a small and insignificant occupier of space; yet it is pregnant with a magnificent and powerful life-giving force.

In recovery, it is important for us to remember that it is God who gives and grows our faith. Zechariah 4:10 says "Do not despise this small beginning, for the eyes of the Lord rejoices to see the work begin." *(The Living Bible)* Lacking optimism, we focus on the teeny weenie bits of faith we have and stress out when we are not childlike in our faith.

Doubt and worry cripple us, and we must remember the phrase "Easy does it!" Even though we have experienced amazing changes in our lives, we struggle with the idea of faith and want more than anything else for our lives to continue to change and get better. Patience is not something we welcome, and we want everything right now.

When we don't immediately get what we want, we become full of doubt, worry, stress, and strife and think God doesn't care about us. Gloom and doom may overwhelm when we focus our attention on our wants or unmet needs. We're afraid that we will never have a better job, someone to love us, or a decent place to live.

However, Step Two has awakened us to the realization that we need a complete spiritual overhaul, and we need to stop focusing on our lack of faith, failures of the past, and hopeless outlook on the future. Step Two reshapes our thinking so that we begin to believe God might actually love us and want to give us peace.

Imagine the scene of God rejoicing, dancing, singing, and calling to His host of angels to bring the best food and drink to celebrate the reality that we are coming to believe! He doesn't care how small our little mustard seed of faith is because He is glad, and His heart is full that we are even contemplating that He loves us!

Think about it: angels rejoice and celebrate because we are coming to believe that God can and will continue to restore our lives. Yes, hard times will come, but God, our greatest champion, is doing for us what we cannot do for ourselves.

God, let my faith grow within each second, minute, and hour that passes. Continue to show me the way as I long to know You more and help me feel Your presence as an all-consuming heart experience. Today, the mountain is my addiction. Let the faith, authored by You, move it and cast it into the sea according to Your good and holy will. Amen!

✝

Day 26: *Love Resides Where Anger Burned*

"Yeshua said to him, 'Go! Your faith has made you well.' Instantly he
regained his sight and began following Yeshua down the road."
Mark 10:52.
(Tree of Life Version)[14]

Step One and Step Two have shown us that in order to
recover and experience peace, we must come to know a faith in
a power greater than ourselves — a power who loves and cares
for us. There are countless numbers of people who have left the
Twelve Step program because they have not been able to
encounter the God whose very character is love.

However, that does not need to be our fate because when
we listen, we will hear the call of Jesus in the deepest part of our
hearts. No other response will satisfy but to follow His call
without reservation. We may not actually hear His voice in the
air around us, but instead hear it echoing within each beat of our
heart.

Impatiently we think something is wrong if we don't
immediately feel His presence. Expectations can interfere with
our awareness of God and we think He should say something
we can understand yet also wonder what He would say if He
were to speak to us.

In our addiction, we attempted to control everything, and
in recovery we are learning that we cannot successfully control
anything! When we try to create a god of our own
understanding, we cheat ourselves out of experiencing the
magnificence of who God is. Just like the blind man, Jesus has

---

[14] *Tree of Life Version*, (Baker: 2016)

given us sight so that our lives once torn apart would be healed through surrender! As we stay clean and sober, it's not hard to see that we were every bit as desperate as the blind man. We could not see the addiction that churned beneath the surface of our consciousness. Today, we have the ability to see how the sun rises on our recovery, and our faith is new every morning. Jesus continues to light the way on the path of our recovery.

Today we are aware, awake, and cannot easily dismiss the notion that God has shown us He is jealous for us and will do all that is within His power to keep us close. Our only response is to give over to Him everything that we are and hope to be.

Breathing a sigh of relief, we are finally able to believe that He wants good things for us and are amazed that hope is slowly replacing the feelings of depression, hopelessness, and pain. Addiction had caused us to lose our way and closed us off from the wondrous things that God can do.

Today love resides where anger used to burn. We are starting to live in the love and beauty we find in the Master of our faith. In the hidden corners of our hearts, the light of His love bubbles, and we feel the source of all life. All we can see is hope.

God, today let my eyes be on Your wondrous face; let me see You! Let me look long, deep, and lovingly at all You are and the beauty of Your majesty. For God, I know my thirst can only be quenched in You.

✝

Day 27: *The Ignorance of Hope*

"He said, 'But who do you say I am?' Simon Peter answered, 'You are the Messiah, the Son of the living God.'" Matthew 16:15–16
(The Living Bible)
Suggested Reading: *Alcoholics Anonymous Big Book,* pgs. 47–48

There are those in the Christian community who would say "coming to know a God of your own understanding" is heretical nonsense and that a person is in danger of eternal damnation if they must manufacture their own God. While it is true that at some point in our recovery our concept of God must align with the truth of who God is according to the Bible, *everyone* begins their journey of coming to know God from the point of ignorance.

Our ignorance is hopeful as we journey to believe in a God who is alive, relevant, and longs to make us well. Our hope is to begin to live again and have the pains of this world subside. We know nothing else will be able to make that happen because we have tried everything to make ourselves well.

Step Two shows us that we must come to personally and intimately know a kind, loving God. It is important that we do not shortchange ourselves and settle for another person's understanding of God. Instead we must experience God ourselves in a real, powerful, and personal way. Our experience must be with a God who reaches out His hand and places it on our shoulders and says, "Follow Me." Our relationship with God must have deeper meaning: God must be real, alive, active, relevant, powerful, and able to thwart the enemy that waits patiently weaving his webs of the pain as he plots and plans to trash our lives once again.

Many of us have been anointed with oil, prayed over, had demons cast out, and faithfully attended Sunday church services in an effort to be unchained from the evil grip of addiction. Although these biblical methods can be transformative, they have no lasting value unless we come to know the God who loves, cares, and nurtures us in our faith-walk. No one else can believe in God for us.

We must research and find out who this God is by studying the Bible on our own and offering up prayers of hope and faith. We will find "God, who said 'Let the light shine out of darkness,' has made his light shine in our hearts to give us the light of the knowledge of God's glory displayed in the face of Christ" (2 Corinthians 4:6).

No longer will we be ashamed of our past because we are beginning to recognize that our failures allowed God's strength and power to rule over our weakness.

God, help me let go of my warped and twisted understanding of who You are. I want to know You anew and experience the faith of Your goodness, love, commitment, and power. God, help me know You more. Open my heart and mind so that I might let You in.

Day 28: *Wobbly Faith*

"Who is a God like you, who pardons sin and forgives the transgression of the remnant of his inheritance? You do not stay angry forever but delight to show mercy. You will again have compassion on us; you will tread our sins underfoot and hurl all our iniquities into the depths of the sea." Micah 7:18–19.

Equipped with feelings, emotions, likes, and dislikes, we are uniquely, beautifully, and perfectly created in the image of God. The most profound of our God-like characteristics is the ability to forgive. For some of us this is easier and for others it is more difficult. Time and again we have rebelled and disobeyed God's direction, and we've repeatedly experienced the consequences for our disobedience.

But despite our tendency to wander off by ourselves and fall flat on our faces, God always forgives when we come to Him with our hat in hand and ask Him to forgive and help us obey Him in the future. Beautifully and artfully fashioned by God, we are able to love because He loved us, and we can forgive because He first forgave us.

The God of our faith does not require us to kneel down and face the north, east, west, or south four times per day, nor does our God require us to perform blood sacrifices in order to gain His forgiveness or approval. Our God is the God of mercy, hope, strength, and love. He is a God who delights in spending time with us and He wants us to know more about who He is!

We are his dearly beloved children—set above all other beings in the heavenly realms because Jesus came to earth and died for our sins and created a way for us to experience an intimate and beautiful relationship with God. God extended to us extravagant mercy and promises that we are His dearly beloved children who we will spend eternity with Him.

Even though man continues to pull out all the stops to create and offer a god who is attractive and fashioned in our likeness, that god is powerless and incapable of loving us because only God is the source of love. God is delighted by us, and we experience Him in new ways every day as He grants us the ability to live our lives differently and the power to do His will.

He encourages us to approach the throne of His glory so we can have a unique, personal, and love-inspiring relationship with the God of the universe. God is not dead; He is a living, breathing, active God who is delighted when we begin to move toward Him in faith and seek His friendship with a deep-down-in-our-heart desire to know Him more.

He is our Father who watches His beloved child take her first wobbly steps and trusts that she will know when to reach out and ask for help. He watches as she stumbles, falls, and gets back up again. And He is delighted when she holds out her chubby little arms and walks toward Him in faith trusting that He will catch her lest she falls.

God, as I walk toward You today in faith, let all my actions delight you. God, as I wobble toward You in fear with little faith, help me come to know You as the merciful, forgiving, loving, and delighted God You are.

✝

Day 29: *Heavenly Realms and the Twilight Zones*

"Praise be to the God and Father of our Lord Jesus Christ, who has blessed us in the heavenly realms with every spiritual blessing in Christ. For he chose us in him before creation of the world to be holy and blameless in his sight. In love he predestined us for adoption to sonship through Jesus Christ, in accordance with his pleasure and will." Ephesians 1:3-5.

This scripture may tempt us to envision the heavenly realms as a sci-fi thriller complete with weird figures and hard to believe bizarrely twisted *Twilight Zone* plots. In the initial phases of our recovery, reading the Bible leaves us thinking this is stuff only a vivid and overactive imagination could whip up. Standing on the fringes of coming to believe, we will have moments where we scoff at the stories we read and the precepts we learn. We will puff ourselves up because this stuff of fairy tales has never helped us!

It is important not to be too hard on ourselves in our times of disbelief—we need to give ourselves a break. If Step Two has taught us anything it is that God is greater than our lack of belief and moment by moment He is presenting Himself more fully in our lives!

If we think about a scripture and let it sink in for just a moment, we might feel the Spirit begin to stir in our hearts. God spoke into existence the heavens and earth and the countless numbers of species and within each species multiple variations. But the most interesting aspect of God's creative and transformative power is that He did not just speak us into existence—He fashioned us with His own hands!

How can we not believe in this extraordinary and powerful source of all mercy and love? It is beginning to take more energy to not believe than to believe. Evolution just isn't a grand enough concept to explain all that is in us and around us! We are blessed with not just one spiritual blessing, but with *every* spiritual blessing! He has blessed us in ways we can never know or begin to understand because God is far above us in knowledge, love, and personhood.

But God makes Himself known to us as we begin to believe and trust in Him and set out on a course to surrender our lives completely to Him. God chose us even before He created the world—before time began.

Our pain and our past failures may make it difficult for us to accept that God the Father loves us this much. But one day, one prayer, one Bible verse, and one meditation at a time, we will learn that God's love for us knows no bounds. In a world where rejection, abandonment, and the fear of being alone prevail, we must strive to keep our hearts centered on the truth that we are loved, wanted, and belong. We are the chosen and beloved children of God.

God, thank You for choosing me as Your own. God, let my response be to accept Your love and receive your gift and take the journey to know You as my own true Father.

Day 30: *Tested in the Furnace*

"See, I have refined you, though not as silver; I have tested you in the furnace of affliction." Isaiah 48:10

Suggested Reading: *Alcoholics Anonymous Big Book, page xxvii.*

If anyone feels the hot burn of refinement, it's us! Even so, we still don't feel comfortable in church and find ourselves more comfortable in the Twelve-Step meetings. We still seethe in resentment and feel like an outsider rather than an insider.

There is no doubt, though, that if we stay on the fringes of recovery, we're unlikely to come out from under the hold addiction has on us. Intellectually we know that Jesus has set us free from condemnation and judgment, but we are discouraged because we have *less* than a mustard seed of faith.

It is creepy-crawly awful that we just can't seem to believe we are forgiven, which then makes it even more difficult to forgive ourselves! But when we are together with other people just like us, we begin to believe this common thread of affliction gives us hope for freedom.

Intimately, we engage in the fellowship and feel understood by our new friends in the Twelve-Step programs and wonder why we couldn't seem to find this in the church. It is sad that this is our experience, but it is important we don't fall into the trap of thinking God's people have failed us. Instead, let us be grateful that He has provided us with people who intimately understand our struggles and are able to help us stay sober one more day.

Our common experience of being at the very brink of death knits and binds us together with new hope for our lives. It is miraculous and we are in awe that God's own hand reached out to us and snatched us from the misery of being alive yet dead! The memories of our torturous existence begin to recede because we have new experiences of hope.

The initial process of what we call "coming to believe" is worthy of a response and we grasp on to each other as if our very lives depend upon it! The modern church, while good for our continued and edifying relationship with the body of Christ, cannot replace what we have so graciously been given in the Twelve Step program. Likewise, the Twelve Step program cannot replace the body of Christ, and we will find as our recovery work progresses how much we need them.

God, today I am so grateful, even in the midst of suffering, for all that You have delivered me from. Lead me to be grateful as well for what You have delivered me to — the body of Christ, the assembly of sinners made righteous. My Twelve Step friends understand me; the church understands You. Thank You, God, for giving me both.

Step Three

"Made a decision to turn our will and lives over to the care of God as we understood him."
Alcoholics Anonymous

Day 1: *He is Faithful and True*

Suggested Reading: *Alcoholics Anonymous Big Book*, pgs. 60–61.

Passed down from generation to generation, addiction is not a new phenomenon, and the grimmest of reapers has left wreckage and terror in its wake. Failed treatment attempts, the courts giving us our children back only for us to relapse, or treatment court failures. We blame the Twelve-Step programs and the community listens.

It is now common to hear that the Twelve-Step program doesn't work. The courts, social workers, and medical communities on the front lines of trying to help us battle our addiction think pharmacological drug replacement therapies are the only thing that will save us!

Active addiction shows itself in a myriad of ways and we may be diagnosed with a personality disorder or an organic mental health problem such as bipolar, schizophrenia, depression, anxiety, or the like. While we may have one of these disorders, it may also be true that our addiction mimics or intersects with the symptomology of addiction.

But time and again, those who cross through the doors of the Twelve-Step program and cannot seem to recover have blamed everyone and everything for their failure to follow even the simplest of suggestions. They have been unwilling to be open and honest, unwilling to listen, learn, and follow the simple suggestions of recovery. Refusing to admit powerlessness and unmanageability. they completely miss the first step forward in recovery.

While we understand why professionals and family members are desperate to alleviate our suffering, they lack the power to do so (even with manufactured designer drugs). No human knows our suffering more than we do, and Step Three prepares us to surrender our lives over to God who can and will change us *if we seek Him.*

The journey into Step Three is a wondrous, eye-opening, and powerful experience for people who suffer from addiction. We know firsthand that trying to live our lives separated from God is disastrous. Step Three encourages us to glance at our yesterdays and more importantly to lean forward into the hope of surrender.

Being in control is exhilarating and being in charge of our destiny thrilling (at least when things go well). The non-addicted individual may chart their own destiny without God, and it may work out well; however, for us, the positive results of a self-directed and God-less life are short-lived.

We will find in recovery that we may, with a flower in our mouths, successfully and artfully dance the tango of self-will for a time; however, experience shows that we will eventually falter. When our dance of self-will shoves us face-first to the dance floor, the patient, loving and kind God we have come to know will show us He has not abandoned us and will use our failure to teach us to trust Him.

God, there are so many times I rely on my own knowledge rather than bringing my problems to You. But You, God, are faithful and true and always seek to teach me more of who You are and that that I can trust and depend upon Your goodness, grace, and truth.

✞

Day 2: *He is Our Only Defense*

"Why do you call Me 'Master, Master' and do not do what I say? Everyone who comes to Me and hears My words and does them, I will show you what he is like. He is like a man building a house, who dug deep and laid a foundation on the rock. And when a flood came, the torrent burst against that house but could not shake it, because it had been well built. But the one who hears yet does not do is like a man who built a house upon land without a foundation. When the torrent burst against it, immediately it collapsed – and the destruction of that house was great!" Luke 6:46–49
(Tree of Life Version)

Self-reliance, creative life-planning, and the best counseling might give us a sandbag or two when torrents of life hammer up against our human resources and overtake what we had believed to be fail-proof defenses. But defeat will hammer us until we realize the only defense against our addiction is God. We are becoming convinced that we can't, God can. We are left with no other choice but to trust Him to protect and guide us.

In active addiction we were plagued with delusional thinking, repeated failures, and hearts that seemed like they would never heal. However, we now are in the process of accepting and surrendering to God and beginning to recognize Him as the victor in the spiritual battle for our lives.

In nature, it is an awesome and powerful thing to watch a raging river that is out of control wash the foundation out from under a structurally sound building. The building collapses like a deck of cards and all you can see are boards descending into and then thrusting upwards through the torrents of water, eventually disappearing from sight. It is a grim and powerful representation of the recovering person's failure to grasp the foundations of recovery. The storms of life will come, and countless people will be sucked under the power and devastation of their addiction. Recovery is never a perfect process and relapse may follow periods of success. Yet, our hope and confidence in God has shown us that while storms may come, they will always pass — sometimes quickly and sometimes excruciatingly slowly.

It is a blessing to see our recovery friends moving successfully through life, growing, changing, accumulating material things, and acquiring beautiful families. We should not be surprised when all of a sudden the typhoon of active addiction sweeps away everything accumulated and held dear.

Addiction is patient; it is cunning, and it baffles us because it is spiritual warfare that cannot be defeated by man alone. We must ask God to help us weather the storms of life as they come. If we remain sober for any length of time, we will witness the devastation of relapse patiently waiting to claim many of our recovery friends. We may not know it until we are told by their family or we read an obituary that their lives were once again overcome by the tragedy we know all too well.

Today, we are grateful that God has chosen our path and guides our each and every step. One day at a time, we will take hold of His hand, placing our trust and hope in Him.

God, today I surrender my all to You. Even if my whole world comes crashing down around me, I know You are in control. Lord, use every circumstance occurring right now for Your glory and my edification.

✟

Day 3: *He is More than Life*

"Then turning to his disciples, he said, 'Don't worry about whether you have enough food to eat or clothes to wear. For life consists of far more than food and clothes. Look at the ravens — they don't plant or harvest or have barns to store away their food, and yet they get along all right — for God feeds them. And you are far more valuable to him than any birds! And besides, what's the use of worrying? What good does it do? Will it add a single day to your life? Of course not! And if worry can't even do such little things as that, what's the use of worrying over bigger things?'" Luke 12:22–26.
(The Living Bible)

Worry just happens. It is as automatic as breathing. But still, when we think about God, we don't automatically think about Him as someone who cares for us or will provide food, clothing, and shelter, or make this pain go away. We have suffered so much we've never even considered that God loves us!

As children, our parents did not feed us properly and we may have lived in homeless shelters, on the streets, or in extremely dangerous environments. Through no fault of our own we may have been assaulted, raped, and suffered under extreme forms of emotional abuse.

The gift of living in today is that we are beginning to understand that the darkness in this world cannot prevent us from coming to know a God that loves us and wants what is best for us. Part of growing up is learning that bad things can happen to good people; that bad things happen frequently to defenseless children — and it is not their fault. We are not alone or unique because different shades of darkness touch everyone at some point in their lives.

147

Yet recovery has prompted us to consider the power of God and that He cares for us and can be trusted to provide all that we need as we process towards surrender. Addiction has been no friend to us and has made our lives more difficult as we've plotted and schemed to meet our needs or make ourselves happy. We have never fully trusted God to help us because that always has seemed to backfire.

When honestly examined, our failure to trust usually involved our failure to ask, wait, and listen for God's direction as we forged ahead with our own plans. Step Three is an action step of identifying our self-centered schemes, plots, and plans. It is a time where we ask God, "What is Your will for my life?" and wait for Him to indicate to us our next step of action.

It is not complicated or difficult to ask God for His will in our lives and to help us survive our struggles. As we pray this simple prayer, relief washes over us and shows us God is in control and our burdens are now His. He shoulders all of our troubles and burdens and welcomes us to continue to pray to Him.

After living for so many years with pain and misery foisted so heavily upon our shoulders that our knees buckled, we feel relieved. God is good.

God, today help me see You in all things. Let my thoughts be on You today and let my actions be governed by You. Send the comforter to me as I wait patiently for You.

Day 4: *Leaning on God*

"Trust in the Lord with all your heart and lean not on your own understanding; in all your ways submit to him, and he will make your paths straight." Proverbs 3:5–6.

It is no easy thing for us to trust and be willing to let God take control of our lives. Many of us in recovery have children and as healthier parents, we are now ready to parent our children. Shocked, we find that our kids aren't ready to let us be their parent because while we were busy using substances, our children had the run of the house or neighborhood and absolutely do not trust us to be the parents they deserve.

Our own struggle to surrender to God and let go of our perception of control is similar to that of our children. We exclaim (whine or cry) with great emotion that we have "trust issues" from years of people betraying, abusing, lying to, and mistreating us. The process of surrender is thwarted as we hold onto these grievances; the pain impedes our progress to even remotely begin to trust God or even learn what trust is all about.

However, pain is a great motivator, and driven by difficulty, we find ourselves at the threshold of Step Three contemplating how we came to trust ourselves instead of God. As hard as it is for us to lean on God, we believe that without Him we are insufficiently defended or protected from the cruel and twisted nature of our addiction.

"Easy does it" as we allow the journey of hope to take hold in our hearts. We are beginning to believe that Jesus lives in our hearts and is wonderfully and powerfully capable to guide us as we surrender our will to Him.

No longer will we allow our former negative man-made experiences with religion blind us to the truth of who Jesus is and wants to be to us. It no longer matters that we spent so many years driven and haunted by the very demons of our addiction and surrendered to the hopeless state of self-without-God.

Today we know that God loves and cares for us. We have picked ourselves up and dusted off the things of this world, running straight into the arms of our Father. What a blessing it is to shake off our hurts, disappointments, and betrayals and believe that there is no situation, problem, or concern too big for our God to handle.

Lord, today I surrender my thoughts, ways, self-inspired hopes, and dreams because I desire Your will and not my own. Help me, Lord, to continue on this journey toward You. I know without a doubt that without You I have no hope, and I want to experience the truth that with You all things are possible.

Day 5: *Run to God!*

Suggested Reading: *Alcoholics Anonymous Big Book, pg. 60.*

Self-will is a lot like the teeter-totter we all played on when we were children. There were ups and downs, and we enjoyed the game, squealing with glee as we soared up and then came down.

Yet, we also experienced some pain. When someone climbed off the other end of the teeter-totter while we were up in the air, we were sent crashing down to the ground, and our back ends got sore!

Recovery requires that we surrender our lives to the care of God and lay down our will. For many of us, this is easy because we still remember the sting and pain of addiction. For others, surrender is a slower process because we still try to influence outcomes.

Sometimes our self-will may be rewarded, and we are blinded by our amazing intelligence and craftiness. We are inspired to continue on in our self-seeking and selfish ways because there has been a payoff and a gain. We weave and wind our way through life – and may even be convinced we are doing the Almighty's work.

Then BAM! All of a sudden everything we had manipulated and influenced – positive and negative alike – falls down around us like wet confetti. Our spirits are damaged, sometimes we feel irreparably so, and we become desolate and despondent, or go to the other extreme, becoming angry and lash out at God for letting this happen!

The negative results of the self-will-run-riot can be a great motivator. After our initial temper tantrum, surrender moves us to search our hearts and honestly review how our actions have produced the painful heartache in our lives. We don't even have to think about it as we pray and ask God to forgive us for rejecting His will.

It is during this time of reflection and repentance that God continues to help us work out our faith and salvation in Him. He is doing a work in us and perfecting us as His dearly loved and cared-for children. It is during these times we realize that His will is much better than our own and we want more and more of God in our lives.

God, today let my heart and mind be focused on what You would have me do. Father, help me be aware of the self-centered thinking so I might be of use to You today. I long to do Your will because God, I want to know You more and experience Your will instead of my own.

✚

Day 6: *Growing Up is Hard to Do*

"The Lord is a refuge for the oppressed, a stronghold in times of trouble. Those who know your name trust in you, for you, Lord, have never forsaken those who seek you." Psalm 9:9–10.

Once we turned eighteen, most of us were firmly convinced our parents could no longer tell us what to do, and we shouted with glee knowing our lives would be without trouble. We were free at last! We could buy cigarettes, smoke, and legally make decisions for ourselves. Those interfering adults just needed to leave us alone (unless we needed money or a new phone) so we could make our way in life.

This experience is even more profound for those of us who experienced childhood trauma, loss, grief, or parental abandonment. We basked in the heady aroma of freedom and struck out on our own to create life anew from scratch. Soon, though, we found that we must have a job to support ourselves and with it came a boss—someone who frequently told us what to do and when and how to do it.

While we may be in charge of what we eat, when we eat it, whether we smoke, drink, have sex or use drugs, whatever we do involves making a choice. Each decision we make requires follow-through, commitment and has consequences.

People who don't have addiction problems also struggle with growing up, but for us it seems to be a gigantic struggle! Addiction is an interfering and powerful force that convinces us we don't need anyone, or anything to tell us what to do.

For those of us who had parents that neglected us, we learned never to depend on anyone because we were constantly disappointed. In recovery, it doesn't take us long to learn that self-sufficiency is a lie and all we have to do is look at our scrapes and bruises from trying to go at this thing alone.

Despite the fact that we continue to struggle with doing things our way, God's promises will never disappoint, and He will never abandon us even if we abandon Him. He patiently waits for us to realize that when we live in self-will, life invariably ends in defeat.

Living without God is lonely, and people can't fill our place of deep longing. No one needs to convince us that we are empty. Gaining confidence in the recovery process, we begin to trust in God and realize that even when we fall down, He is there when we get back up.

We are learning that He will never turn from us in our time of need and will always welcome us home as we walk toward Him with heartfelt surrender.

Father, today I bring to You all my hurts. God, I am firmly convinced a life without You is meaningless and fraught with needless pain. I offer up all things in my life to You to do as You will. For I know in You all things are possible.

Day 7: *His Son is the Solution*

"My human pride does not like the Bible's solution to my problems. I would prefer to have a Father in heaven who would lift me up to his lap; solve all my little problems and failures, assure me that I am a fine person, pet me on the rump and send me on my way. In this way I could preserve my dignity and be a good Christian, but I would never realize how much I need Jesus. But this is not God's way of dealing with the human condition. God tells me that I am the problem, and his Son is the solution." [1]

The world might think our addiction is a curse and that we are the scourge of society; however, we can see how God is using our failures to change and heal us. In addiction we were immersed up to our chins in pride, resentment, anger, and bitterness, which in recovery has become fertile ground for God to move, shape, and mold us.

We may struggle and resist, but He will cultivate us spiritually despite the fact we're not done with self-centered foolishness. Constantly ignoring His call, we're beat up black-and-blue, knocked down and devastated, and life sends us scurrying for cover. Why would God, who created the entire universe and all that is in it, continue to help us and extend such forgiveness and use such extraordinary power to pursue and make us right with Him?

Simply put, God is out of our league; we'll never fully understand Him completely! All we need to know is that He is good and just, despite the fact we are sinners and constantly fail.

---

[1] Don Matzat, *Christ-Esteem: Where the Search for Self-Esteem Ends*, (Harvest House, 1990), pg. 53.

God remains committed for no other reason than He is who He is!

Even so, God loves us too much to let us remain as we are and through grace doesn't give up on us. He continues to mold us according to the vision He has for our lives. He wants a relationship with us and is willing to go to any lengths to help us change so we will be convinced of how much we need Him.

In times of trouble, we seek comfort in the shadow of His wing, and even though we find surrender and relief, it's all too often that we take our will back, exchanging serenity for what we think is wise. But we should not beat ourselves up because we can't help but be human, and God will always be God.

Throughout our recovery, we will continue to be hampered by self-seeking and crave the wisdom of the world and tangible man-made solutions that seem to work and provide temporary relief. But always these fixes are temporary and eventually they fade and fail . . . again and again.

However, despite these momentary reprieves and setbacks, we are sealed by the Holy Spirit through our salvation in Jesus, and His truth resonates in our hearts. The truth is that without Jesus we have no hope and no eternity lived in the presence of God. As Paul says in Philippians 3:8, all we have is manure; dung compared to the riches we find in Jesus! Why would we ever we trade eternity for dung?

God, today help me see the pride that spurs me on and offers me false hope and empty promises. Let me find Jesus in every moment of my life and every circumstance I experience. I ask that You continue to mold me and make me into who You would have me be.

✟

Day 8: *Live One Day at a Time*

"So, don't worry at all about having enough food and clothing. Why be like the heathen? For they take pride in all these things and are deeply concerned about them. But your heavenly Father already knows perfectly well that you need them, and he will give them to you if you give him first place in your life and live as he wants you to. So, don't be anxious about tomorrow. God will take care of your tomorrow too. Live one day at a time." Matthew 6:31–34.
(The Living Bible)

In active addiction, we spent inordinate amounts of time plotting, planning, and obsessing about how we can get our needs met. In the end, we paid the supreme sacrifice, losing our children, jobs, families, homes, possessions, and relationship with God as addiction took control.

One thing is for sure: we are a strong-willed and baffled by our own head noise—a collection of misfits that find surrendering to a power greater about as painful as walking across cut glass. Fear of the unknown threatens to pull us under, and we hold on tight to what we think will not fail us; we only let go when we are convinced the alternative won't work.

Developing faith throughout our recovery requires that we let go and begin to trust that God will not let us fall. Just a little bit at a time, as we let go and let God, a space is created inside our hearts to experience moments where it is okay not to know or be in control.

Long before we know it, we are allowing the Holy Spirit to become our life-force. As our trust, faith, and confidence in Jesus begins to settle in and work for us, we come to know Him more and more with each passing day. We are amazed with each new experience and are coming to know intimately what "letting go and letting God" means.

Over time, we are grateful and feel ourselves letting go more and more of the need to control everything around us and clasp our hand firmly in His. Believing God will show us the truth, comfort and love us, we are beginning to experience Him fully as He holds us up when we feel the waves of life come crashing in on us. He fills our hearts with joy because He *is* our joy.

Still we will grapple with anxiety, excessive worry, insomnia, depression, and other problems caused by errant thoughts—because we are human. We will be tempted into the quick fixes that worked for a time such as drugs, sex, food, or power over people and situations in life.

Resisting the temptation that nags at our ears, we continue to walk toward Jesus as He cultivates our faith because we refuse to veer from the path of recovery. There is no need for us to worry any longer because Jesus is waiting and watching and will catch us if we start to fall.

It is a relief to finally discover that when we surrender, God does His best work and we can trust Him for the outcomes. No longer must we worry; we trust and believe that God can and will meet all of our needs.

God, today help me find strength and balance in You. I know I worry needlessly about things You already have under control. Help me see You and see Your hand in the things that are affecting my heart with worry. God, let me walk in faith with You today and always.

✠

Day 9: *Waiting for the Blessed Hope*

"For the grace of God has appeared that offers salvation to all people. It teaches us to say 'No' to ungodliness and worldly passions, and to live self-controlled, upright and godly lives in the present age, while we wait for the blessed hope — the appearing of the glory of our great God and Savior Jesus Christ." Titus 2:11–13

Suggested Reading: *Twelve Steps and Twelve Traditions, pg. 40.*

Our initial action in Step Three may have been to just hang back and do nothing with the expectation that God — since He is all-powerful — would do everything for us. For control freaks like many of us are, the dreadful idea of surrendering means we become helpless and hapless victims that need to be mauled if we are to be beacons of recovery!

But, of course, this vision of what surrender might look like is really our resistance toward change. God loves us too much to allow us such a passive-aggressive approach to surrender. There are times where doing nothing and waiting for God to show us the next indicated step in our recovery *is* in reality *doing* something!

Simply opening our Bible will show us it is alive and full of instruction for every situation and problem life may hurl in our direction. Surrender isn't just hanging out until God does something, and we are not mere puppets on a string waiting to be artfully manipulated. God created us in His image and equipped us with the ability to think, respond, feel, and act.

Surrender and willingness are required actions in order to benefit from the wisdom and wise counsel of those God has placed in our lives. We need wise counsel because we don't have a clue about who God is, what His will looks like or how He would have us act, think, and feel.

So, we seek Him by reading the Bible and by trying to hear what God has to say about how to become more like Jesus. We are ready to experience His will for our lives, and we reflect on the countless times we unknowingly benefited from His presence and how He miraculously brought us into the rooms of the Twelve-Step program.

Instead of focusing on our unmet wants and needs, surrender calls us to contemplate all He has done for us — much of which we cannot see — as He prepares us for an intimate personal relationship with Him. What a wonderful feeling it is to walk through life realizing we are walking in the presence of Jesus Christ.

God, today help me see You as I read about You and realize all You have protected me from in active addiction. Thank You, Lord, for inspiring me to live one more day graced by the strength of recovery found only in You.

Day 10: *Ask, Knock and Seek*

"Ask, and you will be given what you ask for. Seek, and you will find.
Knock, and the door will be opened. For everyone who asks, receives.
Anyone who seeks, finds. If only you will knock, the door will open."
                                            Matthew 7:7–8
                                            (The Living Bible)
"Seek the Lord and His strength. Seek His face continually."
                                            Psalm 105:4.

If we are honest, we would be thrilled if we could get
everything we ever wanted and have that genie-in-the-bottle-
three-wishes experience! It is exhilarating when we do
something on our own and achieve our goal and nothing bad
befalls us. We did it our way and everything worked out just
fine. The benefit is that we got what we wanted with little or no
effort.

However, the consequence is we become less likely in the
future to consult with or include God in our lives. Some of us
arrive through the doors of recovery with resources and skills
while others have none at all. Those of us who arrive with few
resources or skills for living tend to find surrender easier
because we have nothing to lose and everything to gain.

Those of us who have confidence in our own way of doing
things tend to struggle with the process of surrender because it
requires us to stop before we act and ask God what He wants us
to do! Surrender finds us standing at the door, extending our
arm, making a fist and hammering at the door hoping God will
answer!

Ever faithful, He opens the door to the good, the bad, and
the ugly of our lives. It is hard to surrender the good things in
our lives because we really don't want God to interfere and fear

161

we might lose something. Even if we've been in recovery for many years, surrendering our will to God may be a struggle. Learning that the best results come to us when we submit to His will, His presence becomes the song of our heart and our lives become better than we could ever imagine.

We can be sure that when we climb back up on our soapbox and think we can direct our lives again; another dose of humility is just around the corner. God loves His kids and is faithful and gracious, and He is also committed to teaching and disciplining us so we can learn how to live according to His will. God will never abandon us even if we step out and away from His will. Always, when we knock at the door, we will find that Jesus answers and pours His best into our lives.

God, today let me seek You in all I do, think, feel, say, and do. God, show me any wrong motives or actions. Thank You for always answering my call.

✝

Day 11: *What a Friend We Have in Jesus*

What a friend we have in Jesus, all our sins and griefs to bear!
What a privilege to carry everything to God in prayer!
Oh, what peace we often forfeit. Oh, what needless pain we bear,
All because we do not carry everything to God in prayer!
- Words by Joseph M. Scriven

The song "What a Friend We Have in Jesus" is such a beautiful hymn and so artfully reassures us that He is our friend even when we are tired, stressed out, worried, or feel desperate. It helps us when we let the truth of Jesus seep into our hearts.

He tells us that He is gentle and humble in heart and promises to give our souls relief, rest, and reprieve even as we suffer and struggle in recovery. He invites us to bring our heavy burdens to Him and will give us hope, encouragement, and security.

Picture Him there waiting to take from us the heavy, weighty, painful, and worrisome things we carry so we can find relief, rest, comfort, and peace. But still, we struggle and fight and go it alone until we are forced by the sheer consequences of doing things our own way!

Repeatedly and relentlessly, Jesus continues to encourage us to give Him our rubbish, junk, and bric-a-brac! Maybe the song should be titled "What a gift we have in Jesus." He watches, listens, and waits patiently for us to surrender everything that troubles us and causes pain.

Regardless of our past mistakes, He comes rushing in to help us because He loves us so very much. At times, we wait to let go until out of sheer necessity we have no other choice than to drop our burdens little by little and one by one.

Once we finally let go, we experience comfort, rest, and relief. We are rewarded by the stirring of God in our hearts and think we're going to explode with the newness of our faith. His word is sinking deep into our hearts and we are overwhelmed with the comfort He has given us.   Even though our hearts may still be heavy with grief, loss, and feelings of hopelessness, we now know that our joy, happiness, and hope are found in Jesus.

Lord, thank You for taking all of my pain and unrealized dreams, unmet expectations, and giving me the hope that stirs in my heart. I want to know You more, Lord, and understand Your ways. Your faith is making me stronger every day as You create in me a new way of living in relationship with You.

Day 12: *Humility is Always Truth*

"Although truth is not always humility, humility is always truth; the blunt acknowledgement that I owe my life, being, and salvation to Another. This fundamental act lies at the core of our response of grace."[2]

Admitting that our lives had become unmanageable requires that we unfalteringly admit that we have tried everything and anything to control how, what, and when we used. These attempts have failed remarkably. Even the expensive and long-term psychological and medication therapies haven't worked despite the high doses of replacement drugs and hours of interaction with professionals.

Finally, admitting nothing else can relieve us of the obsession to use, we were driven to our knees in surrender. Step One has shown us that despite our creative and crafty solutions, we can't stay sober or sane on our own and we will continue to flail around in the insanity of doing the same things over and over, expecting different results (Step Two).

In Step Three there is not even a shred of doubt that it is by the grace of God we have been relieved of the obsession to use alcohol or drugs, food, porn, incessant sex, or gambling. God did what no one or nothing else could. Even though it is our feet that physically brought us to the program (or someone else's if we needed aid), or a counselor, court or family member who suggested or remanded us, we know it is God who must humble us.

Unhealthy doses of pride, as well as the sense of self-entitlement and self-sufficiency have been knocked out of us.

---

[2] Manning, *Ragamuffin Gospel*, pg. 71.

And ever-faithful, God has shown us that all things are possible when we surrender ourselves to His will. Surrender opens our hearts and we find that we are not afraid of humility.

We have experienced humiliation beyond what others could even begin to comprehend, and we are learning that humility is not the same as humiliation. Humility is fresh, clean, light, and effortless because we count on the fact that God is great, and we are small, and we must become less if He is to become more. His will becomes our greatest aspiration and we are relieved as we surrender.

Today, God is our hope for survival and the only power that can save us from this devastating illness. Where once we had no hope, today we know the great promise of hope, peace, and comfort. As we surrender our shattered and tattered lives, we experience the loving presence of a power greater than ourselves.

God, today I owe my all to You. I am grateful that I can admit all I am is because of You. Thank You for the gift of grace, fellowship, and love. I want so badly to walk with You and live my life according to Your will and not my own. Today, light my path with Your truth.

✝

Day 13: *On the Threshold of Grace*

"He was a murderer from the beginning, not holding to the truth, for there is no truth in him. When he lies, he speaks his native language, for he is a liar and the father of lies." John 8:44

"The devil strikes very shrewdly at our weaknesses. He comes at us at the point where we still want what is contrary to God's commands."[3]

Many of us bristle at the notion of Step Three and wonder why we must surrender our lives to God? After all, hasn't He given us the talents, abilities, and brains to figure the way out of our problems? Addicts (people with so much to hide) are some of the craftiest, creative, and intelligent people to walk the face of this earth. We have to be in order for the addiction to survive.

God, *the Creator*, has given us talents, abilities, intelligence, and a brain capable of creating wondrous things — and things that aren't so wonderful. Few of us can claim that we have been able to dig ourselves out from the pit of troubles addiction has wreaked in our lives. Surrendering to God is a non-negotiable step of recovery if we are to survive and overcome.

Only the power of God can defend and protect us from the murderer who whispers lies into the greatest weaknesses of our character. We must be wrapped in a shroud of grace if we are to survive, and we will perish if we stand alone on the battlefield facing Satan and his army of death.

Standing on the threshold of grace, we must enlist God's operative as He exposes the devil's schemes and strategies. God is powerful, able, and mighty! We are willing pupils and must

---

[3] Charles Stanley, *When the Enemy Strikes: The Keys to Winning Your Spiritual Battles*, (Thomas Nelson, 2012). pg. 13.

pay rapt attention as God shows us personally and intimately that He is with us and stands up for us. Satan is a liar — period. His crafty and well-laid traps and snares are empowered by our addiction and he feeds off of our unwillingness to forgive others and participate in our defects of character.

Our only hope is to fully surrender our pride and our ever-present quest for individuality, fame, or recognition. When we find ourselves skipping merrily down the path lined with self-knowledge and self-enlightenment, we can be sure that up ahead the evil one has set a trap baited with our shortcomings, needs, wants, desires, and insecurities.

Even so, there is no need to fear because God promises He will never leave nor forsake us. We are His dearly and beloved children. And even though we don't yet recognize His enormous and vast power, He still guards us jealously and fiercely.

God, today let me fully surrender to Your will and commit myself to Your ways. Help me discern my will from Yours, Lord, for I long to live in accordance with Your will for my life. Show me how to live.

Day 14: *Learning to be Teachable*

*"So overflowing is his kindness toward us that he took away all our
sins through the blood of his Son, by whom we are saved."*
Ephesians 1:7.
(The Living Bible

Suggested Reading: *Twelve Steps and Twelve Traditions, pgs. 37–
38.*

Few of us have walked into a Twelve-Step meeting after we
heard a voice in the desert or on a mountaintop yelling at us to
"go to meetings so you can help your fellow man!" Maybe some
throughout history have had that experience, but not us!

We were tossed across the threshold of the Twelve-Step
meetings after being whipped by the tail of the catastrophic
cyclone called addiction. It wasn't pretty, and the rubble of our
lives lay all around us. Catapulted into the program, we
struggled as we drew our very first sober breath in many years,
awakening to the fact that many years of agony had passed.

Devastated and broken, with the evidence of destruction
strewn about us, we are able to easily submit to the idea that we
need God more than we need air. We are relieved to have been
saved and glad for His presence, eagerly willing to do what
needs to be done. It is a beautiful place to be, this place of
brokenness and utter dependence willing to do anything.

God is so good and begins to restore our lives, clear the
wreckage, and perform the miraculous. Healing becomes more
common than wounding, and our lives improve; the affliction of
self doesn't devastate us like it used to and we sometimes forget
how we arrived where we are today.

We have a built-in tendency to think we're responsible for
the good in our lives and God is responsible for the bad.

169

Thinking we're responsible for the great things happening in our lives, we must keep on our guard and try our best to identify the trap of self-will. When we feel great and life is going swell, we are tempted to stop asking God for His will and direction in our lives until life, powered by self, has struck us right between the eyes. Beaten black-and-blue by this tendency to wander, we may dip into self-pity and the cycle of self-obsessive thinking.

However, Jesus wants us to look into His loving and compassionate face and trust that He has us firmly planted just where He wants us to be right now so that we can learn to be teachable. There is no other source of power, love, and compassion like Jesus! Despite our failures, He continues to teach and show us His will and instruct us so we can live good and faithful lives.

God, today take my will and my life. I am Yours! If I am self-seeking or self-centered, guide my actions and help me see so that I turn it over to You and walk out my day in the faith and truth of Your will.

Day 15: *Denying Self*

"Whoever wants to be my disciple must deny themselves and take up their cross daily and follow me. For whoever wants to save their life will lose it, whoever loses their life for me will save it." Luke 9:23–24.

It is hard to say whether or not we would have attempted recovery had we known it would be a journey of being prodded and poked toward change. Add to the mix the reality that we would have to walk away from our own plans and come to terms with the fact that we had to surrender all of who we are, including our wants, needs, and crafty schemes, to a power greater than ourselves!

Had we known (we think) many of us wouldn't have started out on this difficult journey, but God had other plans. We learned in the early stages of recovery that the hocus-pocus of self-knowledge just landed us in more trouble. And we did not find any sense of long-lasting relief or protection from ourselves because self can't fix self.

Our identity in addiction doesn't work in recovery, and we just don't know who we are! In active addiction, we became the behaviors that were required to meet the very hungry and thirsty needs of our addiction. We are drug, food, sex, alcohol, and/or gambling addicts and through the bitter consequences of addiction have lost our jobs, relationships, families, children, health, and safety.

In recovery we have surrounded ourselves with other societal misfits as we gather around tables, drinking coffee and discovering we are not identified by our behaviors. But we are grateful that these behaviors have brought us to our knees in surrender. We find comradery, understanding, compassion, and hope in the Twelve Step program as we learn from each other. We find it isn't as difficult as we thought to learn to love others who are equally as messy.

Settling into the rhythm of recovery, we find that while it is simple, it is not easy. Our self-centered and "hurray-for-me-forget-you" thinking, selfishness, overabundance of pride, dishonesty, and paralyzing needs must be nailed to the cross in surrender. It isn't like we jump and pick up our splinter-edged crosses! No! Most of the time we struggle under its sheer weight and drag our weathered and weary selves toward surrender because we have realized no other power offers us the hope that Jesus does.

Timid joy begins to flutter in our hearts and step by step — cross and all — we find ourselves strengthened, emboldened, and blessed as we walk hand-in-hand with our Creator.

God, today take all of me, good and bad, and use me for Your purpose and Your will. Thank You for all You have given me and continue to do for me as I seek recovery. You are mighty and true, Lord, and I surrender myself to You.

Day 16: *Praying for Patience*

"Be still before the Lord and wait patiently for him; do not fret when men succeed in their ways, when they carry out their wicked schemes." Psalm 37:7.

The old-timers in the Twelve Step program warn: "Whatever you do, don't pray for patience, because God will give it to you!" Being still, doing nothing, lifting not even a finger is a very difficult concept to grasp and even harder for us to do.

Yet if we are to live Step Three and surrender our will, patience is essential! Surrender means that we stop listening to our seductive thoughts and acting on our own behalf and learn to listen for His voice! We must begin to follow God's directions like a good soldier deployed to fight in the battle of this life!

So far, things are going well for us and we realize that God has already done the miraculous in our lives. He has willed us the willingness to want to change as we work with a sponsor, attend support-group meetings, and end associations and relationships that are dangerous and threaten to snuff out the flickering light of recovery.

Learning to take all of our troubles and heavy hurts to our God in prayer, we also find that the Bible fills and satisfies us like nothing else can. Our hearts stir with anticipation as we wait for Him to show us the next right thing to do.

Most of us have difficulty with waiting patiently and still struggle with the desire for instant gratification. We proclaim, "God gave us brains to think and work out our own problems!" This logic gets us into trouble because we find ourselves trying to control everything again.

173

God's creation of man was pretty amazing; however, unfortunately, we continue what Adam began, and addiction has further twisted our rebellion and kicked it up a notch. God can and will use our skills, abilities, gifts, and talents to get better and help others, but we are learning there is a difference between His will and ours.

It is the difference between understanding His will and our own that sends us spinning off-kilter into dangerous territory. Spending time reading about who God is and how He works and praying for His will in our lives helps calm our fears. We are amazed at the wondrous work He is doing and want more.

God, today take my will, take my hands and feet, and use them for others. Let the glory of Your will fall on my life as I wait patiently to see You at work in my recovery.

Day 17: *He is Mindful of Our Every Need*

"He will never leave or forsake you. He will give you the strength you need according to His riches in glory. He is mindful of your every need and will provide for each one. Nothing is too difficult for Him, and no matter what happens, He will never deny loving and knowing you."[4].

Rejection is an old and familiar acquaintance and has left a large, deep, and festering wound in our hearts. Whether we were abandoned by our parents, the love of our life, or our children — or it is a perception of events — it carries over into our relationship with God.

If we stay sober for any length of time, there will be times we feel that God isn't listening because He isn't healing us or changing others or our circumstances fast enough or in ways we think He should. We feel cheated because God says He wants to give us the desires of our hearts (Psalm 37:4), but every day we wake up broken in a way that threatens to consume us.   Step Three is bittersweet because we must wait patiently (and we are so impatient!) for God to perfect His plan in our lives. It requires that we trust, and even though we might not get what we want, when we want it, God will give us what we need when we need it.

One day at a time He infuses our hearts with a steady supply of faith. Letting go of fear, we pray for the willingness to surrender everything to Him. We stand in awe as we begin to

---

[4] Stanley, *Landmines in the Path of the Believer*, pg.25.

experience the miracle of change in ourselves and the world around us. The old is falling away and faith fills our hearts.

For the first time in many years — or maybe the first time ever — we are filled with joy. The changing seasons of winter into spring serves as a great example of how the old must die so new growth may emerge. Every morning, our relationship with God is new as our faith grows deeper.

Pain is unavoidable and can serve to draw us closer when we call on Him. There will be times we know He is there and yet others where we wonder where He went. Feelings of rejection or abandonment may overwhelm, but we must always remember that God is faithful and will never, ever abandon us.

We are in the process of learning to trust that even if we don't see or feel Him, He is there! We have learned that there is no other power that can bring about the results that God can — and will, if we seek Him, so we wait with an eagerness to see the miracles He has yet to perform.

God, today I ask for the strength to push on and do Your will. Father, help me see and feel you today in the wind that blows, the sun that shines, and the birds that sing, for You have created all things.

✝

Day 18: *The Wrecking Ball*

"Turn away from evil and do good. Try to live in peace even if you must run after it to catch and hold it! For the Lord is watching his children, listening to their prayers; but the Lord's face is hard against those who do evil." 1 Peter 3:11–12.

(The Living Bible)

Suggested Reading: *Twelve Steps and Twelve Traditions, pg. 41.*

The wrecking ball of addiction has torn our lives apart and left us in chaos with the debris of grief, loss, pain, and restlessness that nothing can seem to fix. More than anything else we want to know serenity, peace, and contentment!

Step Three is a process of unfolding situation-by-situation and moment-to-moment. It may occur in an instant, but usually for us, it pours in ever so slowly as we place one foot in front of the other and navigate our way through the debris that addiction has left all around us. We struggle with surrender, and it is easy to give God everything one day yet want to grab for control the next. While we are willful, it is important to remember that God is in control and resist being hard on ourselves. It is unrealistic to think that we wake up one day to experience sunshine and butterflies without experiencing some discomfort because this is the stuff of fairy tales.

As we play at tug-of-war with surrender and self-will—and our solutions fail—we are driven to our knees. We are driven to seek relief from the storm of emotional turmoil and thank God for His care and attention.

Trial, error, and experiences with pain are teaching us to seek His guidance instead of our own. Little by little, we are becoming willing to wait for His wisdom and perfect timing.

There will be times of confusion and indecision, and it is tempting as we fret and worry.

We may be tempted to preach from moral high ground and impose our own beliefs on others without sensitivity to the fact that it is God who is in control—not us. Negative results serve to remind us that we were playing god. Despite our failures—or because of them—the courage and willingness to surrender our will brings relief rather than misery.

God, today let me give You all of my thoughts, desires, hopes, and dreams. I want Your will in all things and to leave the outcomes up to You.

✞

Day 19: *Sin is Not Our Master*

*"Do not let any part of your bodies become tools of wickedness, to be
used for sinning; but give yourselves completely to God — every part
of you — for you are back from death and you want to be tools in the
hands of God, to be used for his good purposes. Sin need never again
be your master, for now you are no longer tied to the law where sin
enslaves you, but you are free under God's favor and mercy."*
Romans 6:13–14.

(The Living Bible)

With spiritual sirens blazing and the hazmat team on site,
we were scooped up and out of the toxic waste-site of our
addiction. God made Himself powerfully known to us. And it is
not at all difficult for us to understand in a very real way what
it means to be brought from death into life.

There isn't even one little shred of doubt that we were
spiritually dead in our addiction and fast on our way to physical
death. Some of us had actually overdosed and were
unresponsive (in all reality dead) until we were brought back to
life by a paramedic or in an emergency room.

Now that we have some measure of sanity, no one has to
convince us that we were spared to live another day and were
given the opportunity to know the power of God. But the power
of addiction being what it is — that even though we were brought
back to life and have experienced the miraculous — it's not
uncommon for us to revert back to self-will.

The miraculous wears off and loses its luster, and instead of
pausing and realizing what a gift we have been given, we start
looking for the excitement of instant gratification again! The
cycle of self-God-self is exhausting, and we are powerless to stop
this dance of destruction.

Few of us will admit it and even fewer can see, but there is no question we enacted our own power and played at being God. It is easy to become discouraged with this dizzying dance. But crazy as it may seem, we are exactly where we are supposed to be in our recovery process!

Our journey does not end with Step Three. God is laying the foundation for us to discover our weaknesses, temptations, sins, and defects of character so we might discover our hopes, dreams, positive attributes, strengths, and beauty.

God is showing us who He is as we die to self and are reborn into a new relationship with Him. Sin need never again be our master.

God, today thank You for delivering me from the terrors of my addiction and for raising me up from a spiritual death. Let me see You more as I turn from sin and awaken from death and into the life you have for me.

Day 20: *From Self to Surrender*

"Jesus called out with a loud voice, 'Father, into your hands I commit my spirit.' When he had said this, he breathed his last." Luke 23:46.

How often we have raised our voices to God in anguish saying, "God, take this from me! I'm done. I'll never do this again, just make the suffering stop!" Our surrender is not in any way equal to the complete surrender of Jesus to His death on the cross for our sins, but it does have deep implications as we toy with what it means.

It is easy to surrender in complete defeat when we are in pain or the consequences of our addiction are still fresh. Waving that white flag of surrender is effortless because we feel the pain deep to the marrow of our bones. The hot flames of our addiction are still fresh in our minds, and all we have to do is look at the blistering evidence of damage.

Surrender doesn't come easy, and our experience is that the painful storms of life are usually what drive us to seek God's will for our lives. Why can't we just surrender before all of the painful stuff happens? The cycle of suffering and surrender will come around time and again the longer we stay sober.

The process of surrender hasn't changed much from our early days in recovery and seems to become more difficult when things are going well. When we are living upstanding lives, doing esteem-able acts, and making great progress in our recovery, we forget where our grace comes from.

Becoming acceptable and responsible members of society, we have jobs, families, civic memberships, and pay taxes. We are well regarded in the community of recovering people. Judges may seek our advice and opinions on addiction; pastors and teachers tap into our experiences and struggles with recovery. Life is going amazingly well.

It is tempting to become super-impressed with ourselves and think we have done it! We have recovered! Look at us! We're really doing this thing! We are so overtaken by grandiosity that soon we forget that it is God who is in control. We have crossed over from surrender into self.

Jesus was broken, battered, and crucified on the cross so that we could find our way to the Father and enjoy the beauty of committing our spirits to Him. He paid it all so we could have the choice and opportunity to live in relationship to God, with God and for God. His life and His death are a living example to us of how to surrender and how to breathe our last breath of self-will and commit our spirits to him moment to moment, day to day and year to year.

In the quiet moments of reflection or in times of discomfort, this step of surrender enables us to breathe out the last of our self-will.

God, today I give You my all. I commit to You my spirit. Show me Your will as I breathe the last of my own and inhale the essence of Yours.

Day 21: *The Merry-Go-Round of Self-Centeredness*

"The Father sometimes allows difficulties in your life just so you will recognize your need for Him. Not only is God prepared to help you; He is actually calling you to cast 'all your anxiety on Him, because He cares for you'" (1 Peter 5:7).[5]

The patterns of self-will seem to go on and on and on! Just when we thought we had surrendered, insanity returns as our self-will re-emerges. We find ourselves doing the same things over and over again that brought us pain and misery as we choose our own will instead of God's.

The gloom and doom of self-centeredness and irresponsibility have once again thrown our thoughts, feelings, relationships, finances, and sense of well-being into chaos! It isn't until we experience the "Big Bang" of colliding circumstances that we are able to see where we went off the grid.

Somehow, again thinking that we knew what was best, we failed to check in with God to ask what He thought we should do! This doesn't mean there aren't times that bad stuff happens when we are walking in step with God.

The longer our recovery journey is, the more opportunity there is for tragedy or the recurrence of historical trauma. Whether life imposes difficulty, or it is of our own making, surrender is a gift. We cannot control life, and no one wants to be a victim for the rest of their lives. We have a power greater than all our trauma and pain because recovery gives us the ability to turn our will and lives over to the care of God.

---

[5] Charles Stanley, *Prayer, the Ultimate Conversation*, (Howard Books; 2013), pg. 34.

Our little hearts have been broken or we may have been deeply injured by things beyond our control. It doesn't matter to God whether or not our problems were created by ourselves or by others. What matters most to God is that we ask Him to heal our pain and suffering. Recovery is a gift and the longer we live in the miraculous, the more opportunity we have to grow and stretch in our experience of surrender. God allows difficult times to deepen our dependence on and relationship with Him. He is teaching us who He is!

Day by day we are learning to experience a deeper faith and trust in God's character. God is overjoyed and we are edified when we cast all our cares on Him. It is during these times that our understanding of surrender deepens. Jesus suffered in this life and so will we. Jesus relied on the strength of the Father. And if it worked for Jesus, it will work for us.

God, life is so hard sometimes! I know there will be difficulty in my recovery, and I ask that You draw me closer to You during these times. Take all of my fear, pain, and anxiety and help me know that You truly care for me. Jesus, Jesus, Jesus! Today I call on Your name. Come in.

✠

Day 22: *Being Born Again*

"All around us we observe a pregnant creation. The difficult times of pain throughout the world are simply birth pangs. But it's not only around us; it's within us. The Spirit of God is arousing us within. We're also feeling the birth pangs. These sterile and barren bodies of ours are yearning for full deliverance. That is why waiting does not diminish us, any more than waiting diminishes a pregnant mother. We are enlarged in the waiting. We, of course, don't see what is enlarging us. But the longer we wait, the larger we become, and the more joyful our expectancy." Romans 8:22–25*
(The Message)*

Giving birth is painful! When the child decides it is time to break free from the mother's body, there is no way of avoiding it as each contraction urges the child forward into taking his or her first breath. Women say that the moment they hold this miracle of new life in their arms, the pain is forgotten for surely they are staring into the face of God.

Recovery is nothing short of a miracle and we are born into a new way of living. We truly know what it is to be born again! Physical and emotional contractions accompany our times of growth as we enter into a deeper relationship with God and take our first breath of hope. We groan with impatience and are eager for God to fulfill His promises and we wonder why He doesn't hurry up and stop this pain! We know he has the power to do so.

We are in agony, discouraged, and want nothing more than for the pain to go away. Impatience seems to prolong our suffering and we struggle and fight against our lack of power to change circumstances and outcomes as we think they should be.

Surrender requires that we submit and give God our desires, hopes, dreams, and pain and throw ourselves over into what God would have for us. As we grow and change, He fills us with peace and patience. While the freedom from pain and suffering may not happen when we think it should, it will happen in God's perfect timing.

As our faith and hope in Jesus begins to emerge, what a relief it is when we finally realize God is changing us in ways we have never been able to. We are taken aback that we are finally accepting the fact we cannot rush recovery! Now that there is no need for us to rush recovery, we begin to wait patiently for God's will.

We know we are experiencing the miraculous because waiting does not come naturally for us and we want what we want *now*! Our hearts quicken with intense longing for God to come in and for our pain and agony to go away.

We are learning in Step Three that we must surrender to the contractions of growth as we cry out and ask God to relieve us from our guilt, suffering, pain, and turmoil. We wait for what comes next and take a deep breath as we wait patiently and hopefully for all that God has in store for us.

God, today, lead me on this journey of life. Bring me to the place of surrender created just for me.

Day 23: *Strength and Power to the Weary and Weak*

"Do you not know? Have you not heard? The Lord is the everlasting
God, the Creator of the ends of the earth. He will not grow tired or
weary, and his understanding no one can fathom. He gives strength
to the weary and increases the power of the weak." Isaiah 40:28–29.

Suggested Reading: *Twelve Steps and Twelve Traditions,* pg. 34.

Oh, how we make the process of surrender so difficult when it is as simple as swinging open a door! Wounded and wrecked, we come to recovery after battling our addiction, being rescued from our war-torn lives and decades of disappointment.

Instead of judging and condemning us, God promises to set all the things that are wrong in our lives to right if we make just one simple decision: Turn our lives and wills over to Him! All around us are broken dreams and bitter regrets. It's no wonder we used substances as long as we did because nothing else could block out the chaos or patch us together, so we didn't completely fall apart. We are living and breathing Humpty Dumpty's!

Here we are in the midst of recovery being told that we have to learn to sit and hurt if we are to experience emotional growth! We don't quite know how to not look for the easy way out, but we are convinced that when we do, things don't turn out very well.

It is hard to wait patiently for God, and we don't really know what it is He wants for our lives. But we do know what we want and hope desperately that God will align His will with our own rather than ours with His!

By chasing our own will and delighting ourselves in what we want, in effect we slam shut the door on faith that has proven throughout eternity to be dependable, miraculous, loving steady, and powerful. In doing so, we have shut out God who lives and breathes and longs to walk with us in friendship and fellowship.

When we become willing to listen, learn, and surrender our thoughts, hopes, and dreams into the custody of God, this act of willingness produces a faith that endures through the hardest of times. We must push aside our bitter disappointments and stop justifying our selfish motives and need-driven behaviors.

We don't have the luxury of continuing to be bitter or angry despite the fact that our childhood experiences of Jesus were complicated by man's confused actions toward us. Or maybe we just don't like the hypocrisy of those who claim to be Christian.

The fact is that if we want to live, we cannot continue to exploit these experiences. We must come to terms with how we used these experiences to justify our continued use of substances and prolonged separation from God. Now is the time to slam shut the door on cynicism and to stop judging others. It is time to walk through the door God opens and experience new hope, faith, and confidence in Him.

God, today give me the strength to set aside my anger, disappointments, and resentments so I can forgive others as You forgave me. God, I ask for the willingness to be willing.

✝

Day 24: *Coming Near to God*

"Submit yourselves, then, to God. Resist the devil, and he will flee from you. Come near to God and he will come near to you."

James 4:7–8

Action is required if we want to live happy, joyous, and free. Step Three affords the ability and the opportunity to open and surrender ourselves to God. This is a life-or-death proposition, and our survival depends on actively surrendering our lives and wills over to the care of God.

Our addiction has bedeviled us, and it is powerful, cunning, and baffling. It seeks to rob us of every good thing God wants for our lives, and it will stop at nothing until we are destroyed body, soul, mind, and spirit. It prowls about our lives roaring obnoxiously like an untamed and ravenous lion.

Frankly stated, addiction is darkness pure and simple. It seeks to destroy what God has so beautifully, artfully, and lovingly created. In Step Three we realize we are deceived if we underestimate the grip addiction has on our lives. But God is good, and we don't have to experience fear or trepidation or feel powerless any longer! God is powerful and will defeat the prowling beast in our lives.

Gratitude springs up in our hearts as we recognize we can put down the trainer's whip since God is the zookeeper and can silence the roar of the beast. There is no doubt we are headed for disaster if we are separated from God. We must acknowledge that we need Jesus more than anything else in life. The evil in this world tries day and night to blind us, clog our ears, and muffle the call of God.

Addiction is nothing more than Satan's nasty spirit of confusion and he tries to trip us up, causing us to tumble back into our old behaviors. Our addiction is always there in the undertow of our consciousness, and we choose to become aware of what we cannot see.

As extravagantly loved children of God, it is as simple as taking hold of God's hand and accepting the security He offers. God promises that He will never, ever leave us! We gladly surrender our will and our lives to Him.

God, today as I take Your hand, let me draw near to you. Take my fear and my faith and continue to create and fashion my life according to Your will.

Day 25: *Use Me as You Will God*

"Dear brothers, I plead with you to give your bodies to God. Let them be a living sacrifice, holy — the kind he can accept. When you think of what he has done for you, is this too much to ask? Don't copy the behavior and customs of this world but be a new and different person with a fresh newness in all you do and think. Then you will learn from your own experience how his ways will really satisfy you."
Romans 12:1–2
(The Living Bible)

While we are a tangle of arms, legs, feet, hands, and hearts, the stage is set for us to surrender. For some of us, surrender comes easily, and for others it the most difficult thing we will ever do. We are a strong-willed group of people who think we know best!

Even though we still feel the painful fallout from our addiction, we continue to tangle with the lie of self-sufficiency and think that we don't really need all of this God stuff. Not only that, but we don't need anyone else either! People just cause trouble for us!

Yet some of us grab onto the concept of surrender and begin recovery at a breakneck speed and face different obstacles. Filled with zeal, we enthusiastically wave our white flag for all to see and shout from the pinnacle of hope that we need God — and so do you!

We may tell everyone we meet at the local shopping mall about all the good things God has done for us and — not stopping there — what God wants to do for them too. We refer to this as the "pink cloud," which is usually followed by a black one. As the evangelistic wind is knocked out of us, we climb into our car, recovery sticker and all, leave the mall and give the finger to the first driver that gets in our way!

We all come to recovery with different experiences of God. Some of us have had troubled times with religion and others have never been exposed. Our experience of surrender is diverse; yet at the same time, we are all struggling to overcome obstacles, the lack of knowledge, seething resentments, or mental blocks that thwart our attempt to admit we need a power greater than ourselves.

However, we are beginning to believe that cutting God out closes us off from the sunlight of His Spirit. (We hear people say this all the time in meetings.) Thank God for the gift of the teachable moments where we realize there is no other choice but to let go and let God.

We are getting ready to cross over the threshold and into a profound belief where God's presence captivates our hearts. Trading our ashes for beauty, we surrender our will and lives over to the care of God. As we stay the course of surrender, we realize the desires of this world no longer satisfy what our hearts long to embrace.

God, thank You for all You have done for me and continue to do. Take me, Lord, for I am Yours and am no longer tied to the things of this world. Use me God as You will.

✟

Day 26: *Keep Alert and Pray*

"Then he told them, 'My soul is crushed with horror and sadness to the point of death. . . stay here . .. stay awake with me.' He went forward a little, and fell face downward on the ground, and prayed, 'My Father! If it is possible, let this cup be taken away from me. But I want your will, not mine.' Then he returned to the three disciples and found them asleep. 'Peter,' he called, 'couldn't you even stay awake with me one hour? Keep alert and pray. Otherwise temptation will overpower you. For the spirit indeed is willing, but how weak the body is!'" Matthew 26:38–41
(The Living Bible)

The disciples knew Jesus in person, spent time with Him, prayed with Him, and ate with Him. But even they couldn't overcome the desires of their bodies and the need for sleep! We are so hard on ourselves for being imperfect; yet it is important for us to note that Jesus didn't shame the disciples.

Instead He used their weakness to be aware and to pray so they wouldn't fall into temptation. Jesus knew He was facing a horrid death and felt overwhelmed as He fell on His face and asked God for relief. But there was no other way, and in total surrender Jesus obeyed God's will even though it meant His death and separation from God.

Jesus was willing to do anything God asked of Him because He intimately knew God. It defies our pea-brain wisdom that someone would be willing to die nailed to a cross for a bunch of addicts like us. People usually don't want anything to do with us.

It is hard to understand a faith like Jesus had, and it may be even harder for us to believe that God wants to bless us with good and wholesome lives. God knows we're not going to do

193

this perfectly and asks only that we present ourselves to Him and admit we are powerless and that He has all power.

He wants to heal our brokenness and build a trusting relationship with us. Even though our spirit is willing, wanting, and desires recovery more than anything else, we continue to struggle with that "thing" we call the phenomenon of craving that expands across every cell in our body. We have no other defense against it except for God!

He has the power to set us free from the limitations of our bodies and come between our next drink, drug, or drive through the fast-food window. The destructive behaviors are endless, yet the power of God is greater than anything or anyone that threatens our recovery. As we move closer to surrender, we realize He is greater than any situation that may threaten our ability to remain sober. We are grateful and overwhelmed and feel energized more than ever to keep our eyes focused on Jesus.

God, today I thank You for sending Your Son to die for my sins! I am so glad that I will never ever again suffer separation from You. Even though I might experience pain for a little while, let me live in the joy of what is to come in eternity.

Day 27: *Becoming Like Children*

*"He called a little child to him and placed the child among them. And
he said, 'Truly I tell you, unless you change and become like little
children, you will never enter the kingdom of heaven. Therefore,
whoever takes the lowly position of this child is the greatest in the
kingdom of heaven.'" Matthew 18:2–4.*

Childhood is a time of vulnerability and powerlessness, and
many of us have horrific stories of abuse, abandonment,
unhappiness, and suffering at the hands of our parents, family
members, or other adults. Many of us have been beaten,
humiliated, sexually abused, neglected, or emotionally tortured;
our little souls were so traumatized we dissociated from reality.

It's hard for us to trust anyone or anything who wields
power over us and Step Three is just not very easy for us. It's
hard to blot out the experiences of someone telling us they loved
us and then proceeded to hurt us.

We have to work at this God thing and at least try on what
the Bible tells us: God's love is never-ending, and He wants us
to come to Him as little children. But this thought fills us with
the terror of being vulnerable — and we promised to never, ever
allow anyone else to hurt our hearts, our bodies, or our souls.

We may fear that the abuse we suffered has robbed us of the
ability to experience a childlike faith and feel deep grief because
we want more than anything to be able to trust. We want to
surrender to the will of God and not feel such overwhelming
fear. It is impossible to imagine ourselves as carefree children
who have abandoned all things painful and running into the

arms of a loving Father where we find love, faith, freedom, trust, and confidence.

We would in the most needful place in our hearts, love to dance in the arms of God and would trade anything for that feeling of peace, security, trust, and love. Yet, this is precisely what God calls us to do! He wants us to find freedom in the innocent joy of His truth and love.   As hard as it might to put the past behind us and begin to let go of the trauma, abuse, and suffering, our problems belong to God, not to us! Our past suffering is His to deal with. The truth is that those who hurt us as children no longer have power over us. God wants us to trust that He will never, ever harm, abandon, abuse, or forsake us.

God grieves for all that we have experienced and all the harm that people have done to us. He grieves for what we have done to ourselves. Today, we have the opportunity to walk in faith and experience a new sense of trust. Let us let God show us His eternity of blessings, trust, love, hope, and faith.

God, today help me remember, see, feel, and experience the unharmed child that resides in me. God, as I run into Your arms and kneel at Your feet, let Your love envelop me because I am Yours.

✞

Day 28: *He Looks Upon Us in Love*

*"Guide me with your laws so that I will not be overcome by evil.
Rescue me from the oppression of evil men; then I can obey you. Look
down in love upon me and teach me all your laws."*
Psalm 119:133–135
(The Living Bible)
Suggested Reading: *Alcoholic Anonymous A Big Book*, pg. 62.

In the game "Jenga" there is one pivotal piece that will eventually cause the catastrophic tumbling of the entire structure onto the table. Like "Jenga," recovery is a balancing act and God is the one who holds us together.

We come to realize in Step Three that God must be the heartbeat and centerpiece of our recovery. Surrendering is difficult and it may take us a while because we still think we can solve our own problems. We think we are pretty good at recovery and our solutions are endless!

God may be the last person we turn to and we attempt to circumvent surrender so we can do what we think needs to be done. We become baffled by our own logic. "After all," we tell ourselves, "I'm intelligent and have been sober ____ days, months, or years. I'm not powerless anymore because God has given me common sense and the religious acuity to decide what is right for my life."

We may have the best intentions and aren't trying to hurt anyone, but without God in control, eventually we fall flat on our faces and take others down with us! Once again our pride defeats us, and our egos are smashed by the outcomes of self-will.

However, it is important we do not punish ourselves when we become self-driven know-it-alls. Instead, it is important we acknowledge the fact that God has given us yet another experience to learn and grow. The experience may sting, but we know that little by little, God is filling us with the willingness to listen and follow His direction.

God forgives us when we temporarily forget about Him and do our own thing. Instead of rejecting us, He picks us up and dusts us off and we realize that with each failure, He gives us glimpses of who He is and how much He loves us. What a true friend we have!

He continues to point us in the direction of surrendering our will and following His. It is inevitable that we will stray, but our God knows the surrender process will take time for us to learn.

Through Step Three, we become convinced that a life without God is one of confusion, pain, and loneliness! Without hesitation, we become willing to let go of our pride, ego, and self-reliance and follow God's will for our lives.

God, I surrender! I am tired of my own will, God, and am convinced it no longer works.

Day 29: *Hip Slick and Cool*

"Your attitude should be the kind that was shown us by Jesus
Christ, who, though he was God, did not demand and cling to his
rights as God, but laid aside his mighty power and glory, taking the
disguise of a slave and becoming like men. And he humbled himself
even further, going so far as actually to die a criminal's death on a
cross." Philippians 2:5–8.
(The Living Bible)

Everyone wants to be a celebrity! We worship the people in Hollywood, and the rich, famous, and talented as our idols. We even worship people whose only talent is their famous parents, shapely butts, huge lips, designer shoes, and long locks of fake hair. We are constantly looking for someone we can idolize!

It shouldn't surprise us then when we start clinging to people with multiple years in recovery or those who ride Harley-Davidson motorcycles, wear leathers and have a hip, slick, and cool attitude. We have this need to follow and be recognized by people who are fantastic speakers, or have written a book, or are a foremost authority on recovery in their community.

There is nothing wrong with wanting to be around positive people. The problem is that we give to man what belongs to God! Only God deserves our worship, and it is only God who can save us. This culture of celebrity can also plague the church as we throw money at the best vocalists and music directors and create well-lit professional stages adorned with the youngest, prettiest, and most talented of people. But time and again, these man-made attempts of worship fail and serve to turn people off rather than on. It is easy to find flaws in the church as preachers with charismatic personalities are lauded and held in high

199

esteem. The flock gathers thunderstruck at the awesomeness of this icon.

Just like Adam in the Garden of Eden, we have this inborn tendency to elevate ourselves and try to achieve equality with God! It's easy to blame the church, but we do the same thing in the meeting halls, at work, or at the box office. We are vulnerable to following false idols and constantly looking for the easier and softer way to avoid pain and maximize pleasure.

Even Jesus — who is the very nature of God — did not consider Himself equal to God and was willing to follow the will of His Father even as it led to His own death. We are called to be imitators of Christ and as such must surrender and nail to the cross our wants, needs, desires, who we think we are, or want to be so we can serve God and be useful to others who suffer.

It is simple and all we must do is listen to, trust, and obey God. How awesome it is that a society of beggars like us has the opportunity to enjoy an intimate relationship with God. God is making us new every single day on our recovery journey as we humbly turn to Him to meet our needs.

God, humility doesn't come easily to me. Help me, Lord, to understand and live more like Christ with no expectation of worship from others; instead, let me be willing to offer myself up to do Your will always.

Day 30: *Hearing God in the Whispers of the Wind*

"My sheep listen to my voice; I know them, and they follow me. I give them eternal life, and they shall never perish; no one can snatch them out of my hand. My Father, who has given them to me, is greater than all; no one can snatch them out of my Father's hand. I and the Father are one." John 10:27–30.

People who know us realize there is something different about us. If we were to describe to them what went on inside our heads, they would be amazed and horrified at the same time. Constant chatter goes on and on in our heads as we work to break free from addiction.

For as long as we can remember, the incessant thoughts have plagued us. Yet in recovery we are struggling with all of our might to break free from these unwelcome thoughts so we can hear God's voice instead of our own. God tells us not to worry about our lives—what we will eat, what we will wear, where we will work, or how we will pay our rent. This is a foreign concept to us because we're used to having to kick and scratch to meet even our most basic needs.

How can we not worry? Step Three gives us the solution: it is a *decision* to turn our will over to God. God has promised to never let anyone, or anything snatch us from His grasp, and He promises to always take care of us. No longer do we need to scratch our way through life because God is in control and He is greater than the entire universe!

On a clear night, we only have to look at the stars and the broad expanse of the sky to realize how big God is; yet this only shows us a miniscule picture of His might. Nothing can stop our

God – not even our alcoholism or addiction can snatch us from Jesus because we are His!

It is inevitable there will be troubles and struggles in recovery, but faith gives us the opportunity to surrender fear, obsessive thoughts, our wants, needs, and desires. We are becoming aware of His presence and little by little we're starting to trust in His will for our lives. With each experience of self-will and surrender, our faith increases, and before we know it, we are giving our will over to Him!

Like little children, we are training our eyes on God because our very existence depends on communicating our needs and training our ears to hear His voice. We want to hear what He has to say to us as we confide and trust that Jesus will take care of our every need.

God, I thank You for placing me into the tender and awesome care of Jesus! What a wonderful gift You have given me – that no one and nothing can snatch me from Your grasp. Help me train my eyes on You today and hear You in the whispers of the wind.

Step Four

"Made a searching and fearless moral inventory of ourselves."

Alcoholics Anonymous

Day 1: *From Victim to Victor*

Psalm 23:4 "Yea, though I walk through the valley of the shadow of death, I will fear no evil; for You are with me; Your rod and Your staff they comfort me."
(New King James Version)

We really don't like pain and especially dislike having to admit the things we have done wrong. But oh, how we relish looking at what other people have done *to* us! The first two columns of Step Four are easy enough, and we find that there is an abundance of energy to write about all the things other people have done!

But the groaning and moaning begins when we start writing about what was affected in us and then what our part was. However, we cannot skirt around the discomfort because Step Four is a renovation process that requires us to first tear down the rotted structure of self and prepare to be transformed.

Once we commit to this process — pen and paper in hand — we find that trusting God is a little easier. God begins to show us our resentments about people, places, rules, injustices, shattered dreams, and our failures. Staring at the turmoil of shattered dreams, failed relationships, cheating spouses, abusive parents, husbands, wives, and wayward children reveals how disappointed we are in ourselves, others, and God.

It is so important that we don't quit. We may need to pray more often to move forward because we are about to discover what has blocked us from the life God wants for us. We are amazed to discover that our disappointment in God is because He didn't give us what we wanted, heal our physical condition, or protect us from our abuser. We may even find that we are resentful about the "he-ness" of the Twelve Steps!

205

Discovering our resentments is an important part of the process so we can move from victim to victor. Climbing out of the muck and mire of resentment, pride, self-centeredness, insecurity, fear, and self-seeking, we begin to experience freedom from addiction and the authenticity of recovery.

Taking this journey, lock-step with Jesus gives us the strength we need to confront and face our past with courage, integrity, and painful honesty. Jesus has invited us to travel with Him on the road to recovery and find the comfort, hope, and inspiration to live one day at a time.

God, today as I begin this journey, help me see those things that block me from the amazing faith You have for me. Give me courage and willingness as I walk toward You. Let the prejudices I carry with me into this process be challenged because I want to know and experience all that You have for me.

✝

Day 2: *A Faithful and Faith-Filled Servant*

"One of you will say to me: 'Then why does God still blame us? For who is able to resist his will?' But who are you, a human being, to talk back to God? Shall what is formed say to him who formed it, 'Why did you make me like this?' Does not the potter have the right to make out of the same lump of clay some pottery for special purposes and some for common use?" Romans 9:19–21.

It is painful to become right-sized! As we work Step Four we will experience bouts of anxiety and shame yet must accept it as part of the process. Talking back to God, yelling, screaming, or having all-out tearful breakdowns are not unusual.

The pieces of the puzzle begin to come together, and we feel sick as what was hidden deep inside of us begins to emerge. The full impact our addiction had on us, and those who had the bad misfortune to be around us is uncovered and the consequences are a bitter pill for us to swallow. But swallow it we must if we are to continue on our journey toward a healthy relationship with God and the world around us.

Despite the fact we have this tiny mustard seed of faith, we discover we are still angry at God. How could He let us hurt everyone, including ourselves, like this? Conveniently, we forget that we have wills of our own and rebelled against and rejected God, yet still we blame Him, religious people, religious principles, and others for our choices.

Through Step Four, we are discovering that we are holding everyone else accountable for our miserable lives. It is painful to discover—if we are willing to go there—that our primary resentment is against God. How could God, who says He loves us so much that He gave His only Son to die for our sins, allow us to be abused, hurt, scarred, and devastated straight through to the marrow of our souls?

Why on earth did He let our bodies love chemicals so much that we craved them above everything else? Why didn't God let us crave Him instead? We shouldn't judge ourselves for having these feelings and thoughts because this is the great work of Step Four. This inventory of suffering, anxiety, and resentment prepares us to fully surrender ourselves to God.

Transitioning from asking God why He let these things happen, we finally ask God to help us not be so selfish and help us not be wo afraid all the time! God is so Good and encourages us to ask Him questions so that we can come to know Him as a real, present and loving Father.

In response, God reaches out, pats us on our hard heads and patiently encourages us to see that He is the potter—an artist set apart and above all other artists! He tells us to keep coming back as He molds and shapes us into a masterpiece.

God, today let me reside in the faith created by You and for You God! Help me see all You would have me see and become all that You would have me become. Create in me the heart of a faith-filled and fulfilled servant doing the work of my Father.

Day 3: *The Chatter of Stinking Thinking*

"Be strong and courageous and do the work. Do not be afraid or discouraged, for the Lord God, my God, is with you. He will not fail you or forsake you until all the work for the service of the temple of the Lord is finished." 1 Chronicles 28:20.

Demolished — thoroughly thrashed chaos — best describes our lives and offers an accurate portrayal of the powerlessness and unmanageability of our addiction. We have accepted our fate that we cannot use substances and still hope to live happily ever after. However, we know that we cannot do this on our own and need the supernatural power of God to help us navigate the power addiction has over us.

Curious children love to take things apart and then become overwhelmed by feelings of fear, guilt, and remorse as they look at the hundreds of pieces and realize they have no idea how to put them all back together again! Dad's favorite camera, all in pieces means unhappiness and trouble are going to happen.

Step Four can be a fear-provoking and terrifying experience because we "future-trip" on what we might see or learn about ourselves. We know we have done a lot of terrible things and hurt people. But we must have courage and follow the process through from start to finish.

We cannot let insecurity, fear, pride, or dishonesty prevent us from achieving healthy and wholesome lives or stop us from uncovering who we are and who we aren't. At the same time, we wonder what we should do with the anger, resentment, hurt, and pain; and are horrified as we wonder how our lives have come to this?

We are frozen in fear. But fear is a liar and thank God for Step Three! We must remember that God is with us and will never leave us no matter what we have done. If we stop now, we abandon ourselves and reject the miracles God has in store for us!

Despite the disgust we feel about what people have done to us, and we in turn did to them, we have confidence that Jesus is our faith and in Him we stand blameless before God. He understands and encourages us to let Him into our hearts. He is about to perform a work in us that will leave everyone, including ourselves, awestruck at our transformation.

He will not stop until He is finished and will provide all the strength and courage we need to move forward, pen in hand, with renewed energy. We are ready to experience the miraculous, and we believe God will show and teach us the difference between the chatter of our stinking thinking and the sound of His voice. His work in us is not finished.

God, today let me take courage and strength from You. Thank You for never leaving me. All around me I see people giving up and returning to their old ways. God, I ask for Your protection so You can do a work in me.

Day 4: *Wait a Minute Devil!*

*"Save me, O God, for the waters have threatened my live. I have sunk
in deep mire, and there is no foothold; I have come into deep waters,
where a flood overflows me. I am weary with my crying; my throat is
parched; my eyes fail while I wait for my God." Psalm 69:1–3.
(New American Standard Bible)*

*"Wait a minute, devil, can't you see, you lost that battle at Calvary."
K.L. Williams*

We all have a story to tell and a special someone who needs
to hear our experience of how God rescued us from a head-on
collision with disaster. As my husband K.L. Williams shared his
testimony of recovery with residents at a homeless shelter and
introduced the song entitled "Wait a Minute Devil," a shelter
resident shouted with authority, "That dirty, dirty devil!"

His words hung in the air and the rest of the hundred
residents could not help but hear the voice of God's authority as
K.L. Williams ministered the truth and promise of restoration.
The last thing Satan wants us to do is allow God full reign in our
lives and break us free from the terrifying chains of addiction.

Thank God the evil of this world does not have the power
to prevent mercy from flowing in! This doesn't mean we won't
experience temptation and difficulty, but we are on the path
toward healing. The fourth column of Step Four requires we
identify how our resentments have been impacted by our own
selfish, self-centered, dishonest actions and how fear has driven
us so far from God's presence.

Recovery is a difficult process and it requires huge amounts
of honesty, willingness, open-mindedness, and courage. With

painstaking honesty, we see ourselves for who we are. And from our vantage point, it looks as if we've have come down with a type of internal leprosy. We clearly see that Satan's only goal has been to make us useless and keep us far from the grace God has for us.

But the good news is that God is the victor and Satan is the loser! While "that dirty, dirty devil" waits patiently and even goes so far as to dangle religiosity gone wrong before us, we must courageously move past the old messages of damnation and let the pure love of God take hold of our hearts. Arming ourselves with the truth that we are loved and justified by our faith in Jesus, we take courage and accept the freedom, hope, peace, and love of God.

God, I ask for the courage to move forward and focus on this moral inventory of all my resentments. When I begin to feel overwhelmed and want to run and hide from this process, help me keep going. I know You are with me and have the power to keep me safe from the enemy. Thank You, God, for You are mighty to save!

Day 5: *Putting to Death Our Imposter Self*

"If anyone thinks they are something when they are not, they deceive themselves. Each one should test their own actions. Then they can take pride in themselves alone, without comparing themselves to someone else, for each one should carry their own load." Galatians 6:3–5

Instead of "rocketing us into the fourth dimension," addiction thrusts us into the abyss! Once far removed from how God wanted us to live, today our recovery has bubbled up hope in our hearts. We have realized that drugs, food, theft, sex, and other defeating behaviors are nothing compared to the welling-up of God in us.

Even though our recovery feels wonderful, we might still feel like imposters (kind of like Sunday morning phonies) as we compare the person we are becoming to the one we left behind. It is uncomfortable and unsettling, because we feel the absence of emergent trauma and the presence of calm with drops of serenity.

One moment we may puff our chests in pride because we have been sober for a time, but later feel defeated because someone else seems to have recovery rewards. We become jealous of those who have a steady relationship, a new car, great job, and attractive spouse. We've done recovery perfectly — where is our reward?

It is difficult not to compare ourselves to others, and sometimes our disappointments of the past become present in the now. Our experiences with being disappointed or disappointing others — justly or not — still rubs raw within us. Our tempers burn easily since we are still sensitive to the reproach of others. It shoots right through to the core of our being—our new sense of self is still so tender.

If our sponsor calls our attention to self-defeating behaviors that could lead to disaster, we recoil in self-righteous anger, wondering why our sponsor isn't focusing on our finer attributes. Judging ourselves as better or lesser than others, we find ourselves immersed in an upside-down kind of pride.

As we take an honest inventory of ourselves, it is important that we remember how much God loves us. We must remember that we cannot understand fully how much He values and loves us—and the importance of living Step Three cannot be overstated!

We must remember that God is about the business of removing the barriers that block us from Him and defeating our addiction. Recovery is a quest to find our true and authentic self in Jesus and put to death the imposter-self that was born of our addiction.

God, today help me discover You in all I see and do. Reside in my thoughts and direct my actions so my life is focused on Your will, not my own.

✞

Day 6: *Pulling the Weeds that Choke Our Faith*

"Examine yourselves to see whether you are in the faith; test yourselves. Do you not realize that Christ Jesus is in you – unless, of course, you fail the test? And I trust that you will discover that we have not failed the test." 2 Corinthians 13:5–6

We don't like paying for what we've already used (credit cards), saying we're sorry, and being uncomfortable. And we especially don't like being tested! Our lives in addiction can be summed up in one phrase; "Hooray for me and forget you!"

We've taken from others what we think is ours, caring very little for how it will impact them. Step Four shows us how far we have drifted from God. With our keyboard in front of us or with a pen and paper in hand, we begin to write about what our lives were like before and then after we used our first substance.

Patterns begin to emerge, and we clearly see the origins of our need for power and control that occurred even before we left the schoolroom. It is shocking because we had always thought it was our use of substances that caused all of our difficulties.

Yet the picture our inventory shows us is something entirely different: We see how our lack of honesty and overbearing presence of fear, self-centeredness, and self-seeking seems to have always ruled our lives! More than anything else, we desire and aspire to the life that is ours in Jesus.

As we begin to pull the weeds that choke our faith, we feel God's presence and are inspired to know more of who He is. Step Four allows us to discover the truth about ourselves and the devastating and fatal grip addiction had on our lives.

This is not a time to minimize, rationalize or deny, nor scrimp and save in identifying our overabundance of pride. This is the time to take a thorough, bold, and brave appraisal of how our addiction has been enabled to grow and thrive. Honesty must rule as we comb through the corners of our hearts and scrape the memories from the deepest recesses of our minds.

The vague and distant memories of trauma must be drawn out so we can discover how our little hearts were hurt and later gave birth to the behaviors that do not belong in our recovery. As Jesus calls to us, we open our arms to Him and take courage in the refuge of His unfailing love for us.

Father, today help me see the hands and feet of Jesus and hear His voice as He calls me into His embrace. Help me walk in faith as I discover the things of my past that block me from Your beautiful and perfect presence.

Day 7: *Practicing the Life of a Servant*

"Here's another old saying that deserves a second look: 'Eye for eye, tooth for tooth.' Is that going to get us anywhere? Here's what I propose: 'Don't hit back at all.' If someone strikes you, stand there and take it. If someone drags you into court and sues for the shirt off your back, giftwrap your best coat and make a present of it. And if someone takes unfair advantage of you, use the occasion to practice the servant life. No more tit-for-tat stuff. Live generously."
Matthew 5:38–42
(The Message)

Suggested Reading: *Twelve Steps and Twelve Traditions*, pg. 45.

Step Four is the canvas and God's artistic power helps us paint a new life for ourselves. It is the time when we ask God to direct our creative energies and draw from us the pain, suffering, conflict, and anger. We excel at taking the inventory of how others have hurt us and how they need to change.

However, if we are to take a thorough, honest, and accurate inventory of ourselves, we need to put aside their actions because our work is about discovering how justified our own. We must radically shift our thinking and discover how we always seemed to end up someone's victim!

We are finally beginning to get the picture of what it means to remove the plank from our own eye before we remove the speck from someone else's! Too often our modus operandi had been an eye for an eye and a tooth for a tooth, which had a domino effect as we aggressively defended our actions.

Taking responsibility for our own actions is foreign and uncomfortable. It requires honesty, discipline, and humility to see how warped out thinking has become in addiction. The

217

distortion and perception of our interactions with others usually resulted in irrational and fear-based actions that always ended disastrously. Our polluted thinking sometimes still makes us cringe!

But today, we are ready to move forward and receive what God has in store for us. Albeit on shaky limbs, we are walking forward in faith and leaving the results up to God. We are grateful because we know that Jesus has wiped our sin-slate lives clean and now it's our turn to forgive others.

God, I ask today that I hear the still small voice of Your Spirit residing in me as I take this journey into a new experience of freedom. Help me forgive as You have forgiven me.

✝

Day 8: *The Past is not Our Future*

"Don't be selfish; don't live to make a good impression on others. Be humble, thinking of others as better than yourself. Don't just think about your own affairs, but be interested in others, too, and in what they are doing." Philippians 2:3–4
(The Living Bible)

Imagine being the King of the universe: perfect in form, beautiful in spirit and incapable of mean-spirited thoughts or actions, majestic, holding love for all things with the desire and the ability to exist within and around everything created. But then something goes terribly wrong and your once-beloved creation turns into ungrateful wretches because it wanted to be equal with you!

Well, that is our story! Instead of giving God the glory that is His, we have fashioned a crown and laid it upon our heads. We want control and demand that others love, adore, and give us unconditional, unearned praise, and worship. Gluttons for attention, we play god and want everyone else to serve and meet our needs.

This playacting is all about protecting ourselves and preventing the ugly truth from causing us discomfort. But our past is not our future, and Step Four gives us the ability to change, surrender, and cultivate a deeper and sharper dependence on God. God is doing an update on us — an essential remodel! He is stripping away the god we have created in our own likeness — a messy, selfish, greedy, fearful, and self-centered self-god-mess.

And oh, how we are willing! We're sick of this man-made, self-inspired, and self-created idol of a god. We are beginning to see the results as God clears away the mess and

219

prepares us to confront our frailties, failures, disappointments, and insecurities. He is strengthening us with courage to face our false pride and disproportionate sense of self.

At the foot of the cross, we are ready to listen and attend to His will for our lives because we know it is much better than anything we could ever imagine. With Him, we are whole and complete. Without Him, we are a complete mess.

God, today, I ask for Your will in my life. I am so tired of my failures and aspire instead to be of use to You. Help me know You more and hear Your voice as I empty my heart and mind of my own need and wants.

Day 9: *Whoever Does the Will of the Father Lives Forever!*

"I have seen the burden God has laid on the human race. He has made everything beautiful in its time. He has also set eternity in the human heart; yet no one can fathom what God has done from beginning to end." Ecclesiastes 3:10–11

"For everything in the world – the lust of the flesh, the lust of the eyes, and the pride of life – comes not from the Father but from the world. The world and its desires pass away, but whoever does the will of God lives forever." 1 John 2:16–17

Delusion comes in many forms and interferes with our ability to be happy and feel whole. Weird, confused, and unrealistic thinking weren't just present when we used drugs, alcohol, or other substances. As we work the steps, we see how our thinking problems were there long before we picked up any substance.

If we had a job that paid more money, were rich and didn't have to work, were skinny, long-legged, and beautiful (add preference here), we would be complete and the hole in our souls wouldn't cause us such pain; yet even if we obtained (add the want) we were still unhappy!

We see this pattern in recovery as God answers our desperate pleas. Yet it never seems enough, and we always want more! These wants, desires, and needs are felt deep in the cavern of our hearts and the entirety of our mid-region or what we call "that thing."

In the rooms of the Twelve-Step meetings, it is called the phenomenon of craving. We always want more, and it overcomes over all reason, gaining a life of its own. This is why it is so important that we continually work a program of recovery. We must — or it will swallow us whole.   It drives us to resentment, and we drown ourselves in self-pity because we think God, who says He loves us, has abandoned us and everyone else has taken advantage of us!

The Twelve Steps help us learn to identify the phenomenon of craving and the lust for more that drives it. Whether it is the next drink, drug, relationship, burger or slot machine, the steps lead us to the solution. Committed to doing anything and everything, we ground ourselves in surrender. With confidence, we present our requests to God and ask Him to bring our will into alignment with His.

Despite the clutter of our want and need, He hears our desperate pleas. With each passing day, we are realizing more and more that God is faithful.

God, today grant me Your strength as You show me my soul-sickness. I know that pain is inevitable as I confront this addiction that swells within me. I want to please You, Lord, and walk in the humility of Your righteousness.

✝

Day 10: *The Pioneer and Perfecter of Faith*

"Fixing our eyes on Jesus, the pioneer and perfecter of faith. For the joy set before him he endured the cross, scorning its shame, and sat down at the right hand of the throne of God." Hebrews 12::2

Growing closer to God and experiencing a deeper faith in Him is not merely a philosophical concept. In recovery, this is a real-life and miraculous experience! Instead of white-knuckling our way through sobriety, the steps help us throw off pride and begin to understand it is God who is making us well and increasing our faith.

Faith must grow if we are to survive the feelings that will come as we work Step Four. The disappointment, anger, and pain seem to become worse as the bitter resentments churn over and over in our minds. Yet hope emerges as God shows us how our thoughts, motives, fear, lack of faith, and inflated sense of pride had made everything worse!

Because of our growing faith, we are able to confidently face our truth, rejecting the toxic shame and the thoughts of "if only." Addiction wants nothing more than to prevent us from knowing God's truth because in the presence of God, addiction can no longer stand and must flee. It cannot rob us of the joy we find in our new relationship with God and others.

God blesses and helps us begin to experience His exceptional vision of who we are and who we are not: we are not our sin, but we are His beloved children! As we journey on in recovery, we ask God for the courage to confront our actions and motives with honesty, open-mindedness, and willingness. We need His continued strength because we want more than anything else to experience a new life with Jesus.

God has not brought us this far to abandon us now and continues to do a work in us so profound that there is no turning back! We are firmly in His grasp and feel closer to God than ever before. We reject bathing ourselves in toxic shame and self-recrimination because we know that God put to death every wrong thing we have ever done. We have been set free and refuse to reject this gift!

Lord, today I ask that You continue to help me discover who I am and who I am not. Let me see myself as I gaze upon Your loving, wonderful, and perfect face. When I feel fear, help me have faith because I am committed to this journey toward You and want to know You more and more every day.

Day 11: *The Gift of Forgiveness*

"Let us examine ourselves instead and let us repent and turn again to the Lord. Let us lift our hearts and hands to him in heaven."
Lamentations 3:40–41
(*The Living Bible*)

"Just because we are sober doesn't mean we've been rendered white as snow!" This phrase is stated frequently in meetings but couldn't be further from the truth. The Bible tells us that we have been forgiven and our sin is as far as the east is from the west (Psalm 103:12).

This gift of forgiveness springs us into action and Step Four gives us the tools. We begin to dig deep into our past and write about the things that hurt us and how we were impacted, how we responded, or how we retaliated.

Without Step Four, we cannot fully surrender to a power greater than ourselves because we would stay helpless and continue to fight against anything and everything to maintain our victim status. It is frustrating to take one step forward and several steps back, but we realize faith is actualized moment by moment as we grow and learn more about who Jesus is and what He did for us!

As we grow in God, we no longer think of ourselves as losers because we are changing and believe that we are loved despite our past failures. Examining the liabilities of our character has shown us that we are full of resentment, anger, and bitterness and have been dumped on our knees at the foot of the cross.

Many would say what a horrible thing, but instead of being torn apart and broken, we are renewed and hopeful. Sometimes, the harder we fall the faster we rise with a strengthened faith in

225

God. Crushed and beaten by our addiction we may be—but we are not destroyed! We lift our hands and receive the promised forgiveness for the pain we have inflicted upon others. Jesus has smashed our rebellion under His heel.

God, thank You for providing a way for me to know You better as I begin the journey toward You in faith. Help me see all my actions so my faith will be perfected in You. Remove from me any rebellion that blocks me from You.

Day 12: *The Crushed Rebellion*

"So, I say, walk by the Spirit, and you will not gratify the desires of the flesh [sinful nature]. For the flesh desires what is contrary to the Spirit, and the Spirit what is contrary to the flesh. They are in conflict with each other." Galatians 5:16–17

There are times we are nothing but walking and talking conflicts! We want what God has to offer, yet we continue to struggle with the things that prevent us from experiencing peace, love, hope, and trust. Addiction has shown us how on the one hand we want a relationship with God, yet on the other, we want what we want and when we want it!

But this doesn't stop God from reaching into our hearts and crushing our resistance. We are strong-willed and despite the fact that God reaches in and calls us to Him, we still wouldn't recognize Him if He smacked us upside the head to get our attention! Our entire lives have been committed to pursuing that next shiny object and we have put forth all of our strength to defend ourselves against any interference from people or God.

The turmoil of addiction may have given us pause to ask God for relief, but rarely did we ask for His guidance. No one needs to convince us now that we must find a new way to live. But this doesn't mean we won't moan, whine, or complain or shake our fists at God in frustration.

We may find ourselves cleaning the house, waxing the car, shampooing the dogs, cleaning the sheets, and making the bed instead of beginning our inventory. But God is faithful and will continue to nudge us toward change. The chaos and clutter cannot drown out God's prompting and we trust He will have His way in us.

Lord, today calm the voices that are constantly fighting against Your will for my life. Help me fully submit to You. My addiction is death, but You are life! Give me the strength I need to overcome the conflict of self and live in accordance with Your will.

Day 13: *The Sweetness of Change*

"But the fruit of the Spirit is love, joy, peace, forbearance, kindness, goodness, faithfulness, gentleness and self-control...Let us not become conceited, provoking and envying each other."
Galatians 5:22, 26.

No matter how hard we tried, we could never find patience, kindness, goodness, faithfulness, gentleness, or self-control in a pill bottle, a bag of onion rings, a bucket of fried chicken, pornography, slot machines, or alcohol. The only fruit we found was angst, moral decay, pain, anger, resentment, bitterness, selfishness, pride, envy, and gluttony.

But today, we have come to believe that we can receive the sweetness of change as we walk in recovery with Jesus. In our sober moments we are becoming painfully aware that our addiction caused us to become resentful, bitter, impatient, mean-spirited, acerbic, and vulgar. We realize that the peace and joy in the early days of our addiction were soon overcome by its aftermath and all but destroyed us!

As we work Step Four, we see how our resentments destroyed relationships that meant something to us. Driven deeper into our addiction we were deceived and filled with despair because we believed we could never measure up. We thought we were helpless and hapless victims instead of the perpetrators of the unrest in our own lives.

But today, strengthened by our faith, we realize that what others have done to us pales in comparison to what we have done to ourselves. Addiction is a cancerous sore within our souls and our only hope for healing is Jesus. Today we are anxious for nothing but wait in hope for God to heal us through our step work.

God, today I ask You to be present in my life. I believe in You and believe the fruit of Your Spirit can become the gifts of my heart. Grant me the strength to continue on this path toward You for You are faithful and kind and want to use me as Your good and faithful servant.

Day 14: *Purified, Blameless and Righteous*

*"And this I pray, that your love may abound more and more
[displaying itself in greater depth] in real knowledge and in practical
insight, so that you may learn to recognize and treasure what is
excellent [identifying the best, and distinguishing moral differences],
and that you may be pure and blameless until the day of Christ
[actually living lives that lead others away from sin]; filled with the
fruit of righteousness which comes through Jesus Christ, to the glory
and praise of God [so that His glory may be both revealed and
recognized]." Philippians 1:9–11*
(The Amplified Version)[6]

Discernment is a tricky gift and we are likely to misapply it
by turning it into a launch-pad of self-righteousness. We are
tempted to use it to judge the motives and behaviors of others
and must be careful to not allow it to become a tool for judging
whether people are good or bad, heathen or holy. Even saying
someone is a "man of God" or "woman of God" is judging and
the Bible clearly tells us to not judge lest we be judged (Matthew
7:1).

Sometimes our judgement ends in disappointment even
when we've judged someone is trustworthy. We still put people
on pedestals and idolize them because they have helped us rise
up from the devastation of addiction or other life problems.
Although we are tempted to put all our faith and confidence in
them, there will come a time when they will fail and disappoint
us because they are human.

Only God will not fail or disappoint! We come to realize,
after life kicks us in the rear end, that God did not intend for us

---

[6] *The Amplified Version*, (Zondervan, 1995)

to use the gift of discernment to puff up our prideful selves or discern whether people are good, right, or godly and begin to follow them instead of God. When we have used the spiritual gifts given to us by God for selfish reasons, we become blind to the truth. And before we know it, we are in trouble and the shame storm descends on us once again!

Thankfully, our God is good and faithful and loves His kids. Through Him we are purified, blameless and righteous! His instruction and discipline are meant to grow us up to be like Him. We cling to the one true living God who passionately loves us no matter what and we reject anything or anyone else who would take His place in our lives.

God, today give me the strength to face myself. Let me see what You would have me see and know and experience Your love in new and powerful ways. Amen.

Day 15: *Ferocious and Jealous Love*

"When pride comes [boiling up with an arrogant attitude of self-importance], then come dishonor and shame, but with the humble [the teachable who have been chiseled by trial and who have learned to walk humbly with God] there is wisdom and soundness of mind. The integrity and moral courage of the upright will guide them, but the crookedness of the treacherous will destroy them." Proverbs 11:2–3
(The Amplified Version)

Step Four peels away the sticky webs of deceit and enables us to clearly see how dishonesty and pride have impacted our lives. Recovery is not for the faint of heart and requires us to grab on to the coattails of spiritual principles and walk through the fear. We are a demolition site and God is in the business of tearing down our old self that is full of pride, shame, arrogance, and self-importance.

He is vested in giving us wisdom, humility, integrity, courage, *and* soundness of mind! We become increasingly willing to see and admit the truthful tragedy of our addiction because we desire God more than anything else. Instead of judging ourselves, we apply fair and rigorous honesty as we write about the mile-high and two-mile wide wreckage in our lives.

It is tempting to minimize and shift the scales in our favor. But God urges us on to discover and understand our truth. False pride is a stumbling block that prevents the truth from seeping into our hearts. But we don't need to worry about it because God's wisdom will always prevail!

We are faithful, because He is faithful. We love, because He first loved us and are grateful that even now He is doing a work in our hearts. Humbling ourselves, we fall to our knees asking

233

God to restore within us His integrity, wisdom, hope, and courage. God is faithful and will bind the addiction where it creeps and crawls like an evil contaminant.

God loves us ferociously and guards us jealously. We offer ourselves up and lay ourselves down at the foot of the cross because we believe He will heal us and protect us with the power and resurrection of Christ.

God, today I offer myself to You. Show me what You would have me do. God, forgive me the many wrongs I have done. Thank You for the gift of forgiveness through my Savior Jesus Christ.

Day 16: *The Quiet Growth in Grace and Character*

"Our earthly fathers trained us for a few brief years, doing the best for us that they knew how, but God's correction is always right and for our best good, that we may share his holiness. Being punished isn't enjoyable while it is happening – it hurts! But afterwards we can see the result, a quiet growth in grace and character. So, take a new grip with your tired hands, stand firm on your shaky legs, and mark out a straight, smooth path for your feet so that those who follow you, though weak and lame, will not fall and hurt themselves but become strong." Hebrews 12:10–13
(The Living Bible)

It feels so good to give our children everything they want and see their little faces light up with joy, and it is equally difficult to withhold, scold, or correct. When they look at us with their sad and tearful disappointed faces, we want to give in but know that what they want is harmful.

Healthy parents don't want to see their child sad with their little bottom lip jutted out in absolute misery. But we know that discipline is necessary in order to teach our children how to make good choices and live happy and healthy lives.

As we come together around the tables of our support group, we realize that we all come from different backgrounds. At one end of the spectrum, some of us had parents who were physically and mentally abusive and controlled our every move. At the other extreme some of us had parents who gave us freedom long before we were able to make right and healthy choices. Then there were those of us who had parents who tried to apply discipline, but we were rebellious.

Whatever our past, we realize that the only perfect parent is God and we must forgive our parents for their imperfect parenting and ourselves for rebelliousness. God loves His children more than the healthiest of earthly parents ever could and is willing to say *no* to our happiness and *yes* to our holiness. He knows better than anyone what we need and turns the grimmest of life's circumstances into opportunities for growth.

He knows how He wants to use us in this life and is training us up to help others. God is using Step Four to build our spiritual muscle and strengthening us for battle so we can help others desperately trying to escape the grip of addiction. What a blessing we have experienced in the miraculous healing of our recovery.

God, forgive me for resisting Your discipline and Your instruction. Today I open myself up to You and reject my pride in favor of Your instruction and will for my life.

✠

Day 17: *The Chaos of Jealousy and Selfish Ambition*

"If you are wise, live a life of steady goodness so that only good deeds will pour forth. And if you don't brag about them, then you will be truly wise! And by all means don't brag about being wise and good if you are bitter and jealous and selfish; that is the worst sort of lie. For jealousy and selfishness are not God's kind of wisdom. Such things are earthly, unspiritual, inspired by the devil. For wherever there is jealousy or selfish ambition, there will be disorder and every other kind of evil." James 3:13–16.
(*The Living Bible*)

Words and actions are powerful! Step Four shows us how our reckless words spoken, and deeds done have shattered relationships, others, and ourselves. We are beginning to clearly see how they have resulted in bitterness, anger, pain, and regret. Our words and actions have caused us to sow and reap consequences we never in a million years thought possible or intended!

When people have hurt us, retaliation is a powerful temptation, because we feel victimized and unfairly treated even though we may have initiated the situation. Puffed up with self-righteousness and indignation, we feel entitled, and think we deserve the best from everyone and everything—regardless of our actions.

But Step Four is beginning to show us how our actions set in motion our internal chaos and emotional tug-of-war. A picture is beginning to form in our minds about how selfish ambition gave way to carelessness and then callousness. We thought only of ourselves and did not understand or care how our words and actions impacted others.

These are hard truths to accept and we might find ourselves sitting on the couches of multiple therapists trying to figure out what went so terribly wrong! Therapy is good and meaningful to our process and can assist us in our recovery work. Still nothing can take the place of God in our lives.

God is showing us that without Him, we are unable to live orderly and healthfully because chaos chases us here and there. No longer hurling accusations at the world when we don't get what we think is our "due," today we surrender ourselves to God. Step Four has shown us how bitterness, selfishness, and jealousy crushed and caught us up in a cycle of self-destruction and caused confusion.

It is humbling to see how we had pointed our finger toward the unspiritual and damaging behavior of others yet were unable to recognize how our own behavior opened the door to sorrow. Today, with a huge sigh of relief — and gratitude beyond measure — we accept that God has made a way for us to leave the darkness behind. We have come to believe more and more that as our sin flows out, His wisdom rushes in.

God, today help me see my thoughts and feelings in the spirit of Your wisdom. Help me, God, produce harmony instead discord and disorder. Crush my pride.

Day 18: *Vigilant and on Guard*

"Simon, Simon, behold, Satan has asked to sift you as wheat. But I have prayed for you, Simon, that your faith may not fail. And when you have turned again, strengthen your brothers." Luke 22:31–32

"The devil has a deliberate, willful plan against your life. He has a goal: to destroy your body, mind, spirit, or all three. His purpose in doing this is to keep God's purposes from you, deny God the glory He might receive from your life, and ultimately destroy you. He seeks to replace God with himself in your life."[7].

Satan is a thief. He wants everything that belongs to God and is elated that addiction has proven to be an effective strategy. He thinks he has successfully snatched us from the God. He has stolen one family member after another as one generation gives birth to the next and the darkness of addiction falls upon the most vulnerable.

Although addiction is powerful, God is more powerful. And while we need not be paralyzed by fear, we must be on guard and vigilant as we work our recovery program. Satan may influence us and try to destroy us through addiction, but he is not powerful enough to snatch us away from God. God knew even before we were born that we were susceptible prey to the snares of the evil one. He knew addiction would be our struggle and that Satan would try to use it and keep us stuck in the pain and misery of sin.

Thankfully, God had other plans for us! It is somewhat horrifying to see how our family history has decade upon decade of addiction and mental illness, child neglect, abuse, and

---

[7] Charles Stanley, *When the Enemy Strikes*, pg. 16.

toxic shame. Recovery is showing us how God loves us jealously and has provided us with a way to turn from our history and live victoriously in the now as we accept God's will for our lives.

Step Four empowers us to discover how we have participated in our own destruction with our incessant desire to be adored, have our insatiable emotional needs met, or be constantly entertained. It is tempting to always blame Satan, but he really didn't have to work very hard to destroy us. We are the ones who chose sin instead of God.

But no matter how difficult our lives became due to our poor choices, God never forgot or abandoned us. We never want to leave His presence again, and faithfully put on the full armor of God and ask for His protection from the evil one.

Even in the midst of turmoil, pain, or humiliation, we need never admit defeat because God has won the battle for our hearts, minds, bodies, and souls. What belongs to God cannot be shattered, broken or destroyed. Because God is for us, no weapon formed against us will prosper (Isaiah 54:17).

God, today I thank You for saving my soul! Protect me by the blood of the Lamb so I may live with You in my heart and do all things according to Your beautiful and loving will.

Day 19: *The Fear of Sack-Cloths and Vile Bugs*

*"One of the teachers of religion who was standing there listening to
the discussion realized that Jesus had answered well. So, he asked, 'Of
all the commandments, which is the most important?' Jesus
replied, 'The one that says, "Hear, O Israel! The Lord our God is the
one and only God. And you must love him with all your heart and
soul and mind and strength." The second is: "You must love others as
much as yourself." No other commandments are greater than these.'"*
Mark 12:28–31.
(The Living Bible)

There are so many distractions that stop us from giving
ourselves over to the full love and grace of God! We're
commanded to love God not just a little bit, but with all of our
mind and every pounding blood vessel in our arms, hands, legs,
feet, and hearts.

So many of us had negative experiences in church and God
was crammed down our throats. Our concept and experience of
God was been warped and we were afraid that we might fail at
this God thing. Step Four is showing us that our experience of
God has been twisted and our resentments have blocked us from
obeying the most important commandment of all! To love God
with all our heart, soul, mind and strength.

We realize that our understanding of God is clouded by
visions of a God atop a mountain destroying an entire town
because of its sin and then turning people in to pillars of salt if
they look back at the destruction. We're desperately afraid this
God will require that we wear sack-cloths and live in the desert
existing on vile bugs!

Step Four is showing us how our resentments and fear have
prevented us from exploring and experiencing the true nature of

God. We have relied on the opinions of others and failed to learn for ourselves about the powerful force of sin and the restorative love of God. The idea that unconfessed sin creates a barrier and alienates us from God causes us to bristle with skepticism. We do not like the word "sin" and would rather a more palatable word be used.

The Twelve- Steps use the term "character defect," which is easier for us to digest—and we still need baby food! It doesn't really matter at this point which term we use because Step Four leads us to the no-holds-barred biblical truth about sin.

God knows our hearts and understands we are actively seeking him the best we can. God's marvelous grace covers us as we try to understand what it means to love God with all our hearts and all our minds. He is faithful and will show us the way to the love so selflessly offered to us on the cross.

God, thank You for opening my eyes to my character flaws, my humanness, and my flawed heart and mind. God, I want to love You more so that I can love others. Show me the way.

✝

Day 20: *Living in the Harmony of Righteousness*

*"Bless those who persecute you; bless and do not curse. Rejoice with
those who rejoice; mourn with those who mourn. Live in harmony
with one another. Do not be proud but be willing to associate with
people of low position. Do not be conceited. Do not repay anyone evil
for evil. Be careful to do what is right in the eyes of everyone."*
Romans 12:14–17.

It is bound to happen. People will hurt our feelings, gouge
our pocketbooks, prick our pride, damage our self-esteem, or
foist upon us the worst types of rejection! Once the tears are
spent and anger resolves, the first instinct may be to strike back
with the full force of our fury. Turmoil boils up and we want to
make them suffer and to experience pain and turmoil like we
have—and more!

The lover who rejected us awakens to slashed car tires or
finds their belongings smoldering in the fire pit or their clothes
mutilated with an ax! We do not let go of resentment or
humiliation easily, and every sermon we have heard and
spiritual exercise we have done has flown out the window.

Blessing others who have harmed us does not come easy
and it's hard to restrain ourselves from hurling venomous
words at the target of our displeasure! This can leave us feeling
unhappy, disappointed, and filled with angst because we
believe we're warped beyond repair and will never have joy.

Furthering our difficulty, we have no idea what real joy
even is! Recovery is a difficult journey because we became
imitators of the world and didn't really care about what God
wanted from us. We may still find familiarity and predictability
in old behaviors and think only of ourselves.

243

Step Four is such a gift because it gives us the tools to take our inventory and become open to explore our concept of God. It is perhaps the first viable way for us to see God's compassion and the compassion that flows from His heart straight into ours. It may just be our first real and authentic experience with Jesus as the lover of our soul as we gaze upon the cross, invite Him into our lives, accept His forgiveness and then extend forgiveness to others.

How fortunate we are that God blesses us even though we did nothing to deserve it—in fact worked so hard to reject it! No one knows more than we do how hard it is to love the person we became in our addiction. But our God is merciful and saw beyond the wreckage and still loved us. He is an expert at loving the unlovable.

God, thank You for loving me! Help me imitate Your love and live to please only You. Let me mourn with others and feel happy for those who have been blessed. Help me understand and extend to others the forgiveness and mercy You have shown me.

Day 21: *We are Loved No Matter What!*

"Follow God's example, therefore, as dearly loved children and walk in the way of love, just as Christ loved us and gave himself up for us as a fragrant offering and sacrifice to God." Ephesians 5:1–2.

"Do as I say and not as I do!" Oh, how often we heard that growing up. Moms and dads joke and refer to their kids as a "mini-me" when the child looks, and acts like them. We think it's funny when our little two-year-old's have short tempers, act surly, or throw tantrums. Of course, it's not so funny or entertaining when we're in public.

Conversely, we feel proud when our children do good things and take immense pride in their generosity and kind-spiritedness. It makes us happy — as if something we did was right — when they stand up for themselves and others and are intelligent, athletic, talented, or attractive.

But the day always comes when they grow up and separate from us. No longer are they a "mini-me"; and have developed their own personality. But we love our kids no matter what they do, think, say, or feel. We even love them despite the horrendous sins they may commit.

God uses the parent-child relationship to define our relationship with Him. Even though we are hot-messes, God still calls us His sons and daughters. Yet we don't quite understand why God would want to claim us as His children because we have not yet found our identity in Him. We're still buried in our shame and guilt and are unable see who we are in relation to God.

Apprehension may thump in our chests as we begin to write about our crippling false-pride, resentment, fear, and our selfish, self-centered character flaws. We see how they have rippled into our interactions with the world around us. We see the high opinion (ego) we had of ourselves and the low opinion we had of others or we had high opinions of others and low opinions of ourselves (still ego).

The beauty of recovery is that we recover together and not alone and open our hearts to the other precious lives on the same journey. No better or worse than anyone else—including the person on the street corner holding up an "anything will help" sign, we begin to realize that our identity is in God and nothing else. God is showing us step by step that fear has no place in our lives because our hope is in our relationship with God.

God, today I give my every circumstance to You. Lord, I pray that You would lift from me the pain and hopelessness of my addiction and restore to me the joy of my salvation. Let my eyes focus on You so that I might continually do Your will.

Day 22: *First Loved to Live Forever*

"We love because he first loved us." 1 John 4:19

"There is an essential connection between experiencing God, loving God, and trusting God. You will trust God only as much as you love Him. And you will love Him to the extent you have touched Him, rather than that He has touched you."[8]

Our idea of love is twisted, unrealistic, and all about how we feel or what we think others should do to prove they love us. Rarely is our definition of love selfless and pure and void of self-seeking, dishonesty, or fear. We question if we love God because we cannot see Him, and we don't feel that all-consuming fire or passion like we have felt in past romantic relationships.

It is a question we may ask God throughout our lifetimes on numerous occasions and in the different seasons of life as our relationship with Him changes. We can't see the smile that lights His face when we please Him or the disappointment He feels when we do things that push us far from His presence.

But there are those times that we have touched the hem of His robe and He has answered our long-hoped-for prayers. These experiences thrust us deeper into prayer as trust pushes the blood through our hearts and deepens our faith. Trust, faith, and hope begin to transform our warped and unhealthy experience of love because it is now about reaching out and touching God.

We are beginning to attune the ears of our hearts to hear His voice. Maybe it's on the beach as we enjoy a beautiful sunset and

---

[8] Manning, *Ragamuffin Gospel*, pg. 116.

the warm wind envelops our hearts, or somewhere else in nature that brings us into the awesomeness of His presence. In quiet reflection, we discover that He was always with us as we traveled the rough terrain of addiction on blood-soaked knees.

He was with us and lifted His hands out for us to grasp in surrender. Surrender brought freedom as God did for us what we could not do. He saved us from the misery and pain of self-defeating and harmful behaviors. As the misery falls away, we begin to feel the humming of first love beating in our hearts.

God pulled us out from the darkness of death, and He will never ever let us go! He is ever present — in the right now — and loves that we want to know and experience Him more and more and learn to love Him with all our hearts, minds and all the strength that is within us!

God, today let me love You more. Let me trust in You for You have my life in Your hands. I pray that I continually reach out my hands to touch You and learn all the lessons You would teach me.

Day 23: *The Radical Shift of Self-Examination*

"Everyone ought to examine themselves before they eat of the bread and drinks from the cup. For those who eat and drink without discerning the body of the Christ eat and drink judgment on themselves. That is why many among you are weak and sick, and a number of you have fallen asleep. But if we were more discerning with regard ourselves, we would not come under such judgment." 1 Corinthians 11:28–31.

Resentments and embittered thinking must be identified and dealt with as we work to take an honest inventory of behaviors that keep us stuck in addiction. We're tired of eating and drinking judgments on ourselves! It is a struggle, but so is white-knuckling our sobriety! It is a radical shift because we never wanted to consider how others may have been impacted by our actions.

We had painted a picture that masked the true impact of our actions as we minimized them and presented ourselves as victims. There were some situations where we knew we were the perpetrator or aggressor, yet we made some sort of rationalization to explain away our behavior.

Day by day, God is awakening us to the truth and encouraging us to look to Him for forgiveness and we take responsibility for our actions. As we examine ourselves in Step Four, we call on His Spirit to make us aware of the important things God wants to teach us so we can learn to depend on Him more and more every day.

We are natural resisters and try to escape this work, but God is greater than our resistance and will inspire us to boldly and bravely confront what He wants to show us. God has a plan that involves growing us deeper in our knowledge of Him to experience a deeper faith than we ever thought possible. Once dead in our transgressions, today we are alive and renewed!

It is amazing how the resentments and bitter thoughts begin to fade away! We are grateful for the opportunity to examine how our actions impacted the way we experienced life. As we take the bread and drink the wine (grape juice in our case), we experience a profound freedom and extend our hearts in hospitality as we welcome with gratitude the Spirit of Christ.

God, thank You for sending Your Son, Jesus Christ, to die for my sins and make me whole again. I need You today and want to receive all that You would teach me. Lord, I know that I deceive myself and have difficulty with seeing truth. Send the Holy Spirit to me to reveal within me the truth of what You want me to know. Thank You for making a way for me to welcome You into my heart and live again.

Day 24: *Making Room for God*

"In his pride the wicked does not seek him; in all his thoughts there is no room for God." Psalm 10:4,

Like it or not, after writing page upon page of our resentments, we cannot help but see the patterns as an overabundance of pride, paralyzing fear, debilitating self-centeredness, and never-ending bouts of self-seeking leap from the pages of Step Four. We are awestruck at the power addiction had over us and how it blinded us from seeing what was so obvious to others.

Where we had once believed God had abandoned us, Step Four is showing us that He has always been patiently waiting for us to seek, find, and ask for His help. Never has it been clearer to us than it is now how our actions were the primary culprit and responsible for the confusion and disorder in our lives. It has now become crystal clear that our actions heaped one bad experience upon the other.

Instead of seeing things as they really were, we blamed and rejected God. Year after year, we wandered aimlessly. We whined, complained and moaned, and wondered why God had left us all alone in our suffering? Thank God, we no longer want to live in the hell of our addiction! Recovery is teaching us how to ask God to relieve us of our unfathomable pain, emptiness, and brokenness.

We want to shake addiction off like a dog shakes off the water after a bath! What a relief it is to confess to Jesus our pride, self-seeking, self-centeredness, and fearfulness. We are beginning to feel at peace because we know that money, power, control, recognition, and pride cannot even compare to the spiritual rewards we find in God.

Step Four has shown us how the enemy has used self-gratification as a trap to lure us to our spiritual death and shove us far and away from God. No longer do we fear addiction because we know God has crushed our addiction under His heel. He has forgiven us for any and every sick and twisted thing we have ever done. In response, we continue to seek His will live out our recovery perfected in Jesus.

Father, today help me see the self-destructive thoughts, behaviors, and actions that drive me away from You and into hiding. Let Your grace, truth, and light fall on me as I learn to walk in accordance with Your precepts for they are good and righteous and true.

Day 25: *Do the Math*

"So, watch yourselves. If your brother or sister sins against you, rebuke him; and if they repent, forgive them. Even if they sin against you seven times in a day and seven times come back to you saying, 'I repent,' you must forgive them." Luke 17:3–4.

Though we may try, we cannot argue with the fact we have behaved badly toward others and caused them pain. But, the time has come for us to face our actions and prepare for the day we ask for their forgiveness. It's quite a blow to admit that we slashed and burned through the lives of those we loved most in this world!

Yet even in the midst of our shame, we are baffled as we struggle with sorting through and separating out what they did to us from what we did to them. But God is good and continues to reveal to us that in most cases, our actions caused others to respond unkindly to our sordid and selfish behaviors.

In some situations, our actions were in response to how others treated us, but it is a rare occasion that we were complete victims. We are thankful that God has given us the desire to dive into this work and poke our head up through the quagmire of self. The patterns of how our fears and quest for self-satisfaction have heaped burden upon burden in our lives.

God is showing us how unresolved resentment and bitterness have sucked us under into the quicksand of our unwillingness to forgive. As we write about and then reflect on where we were at fault, we begin the process of learning how to ask for and accept the forgiveness we find in Jesus. From there, we learn how to forgive others. No longer are we chained to the past! God is our friend and He has accepted our invitation to dine with Him at the table of His righteousness. Let us clean house as we welcome our honored guest.

God, today help me stay focused on Your love and forgiveness so I might forgive others as You have forgiven me.

Day 26: *We are Justified by Faith*

"Know a person is not justified by the works of the law, but by faith in Jesus Christ. So, we, too, have put our faith in Christ Jesus that we may be justified by faith in Christ and not by the works of the law, because by the works of the law, no one will be justified." Galatians 2:16

Big Book thumpers think they must pound sense into the newcomers: "Call your sponsor! Work the Steps! Do service work! This is all you need to stay sober!" "Thumping" is also present in our places of worship as churchgoers are threatened with eternal damnation if they don't straighten up and fly right!

Religiosity can be found anywhere God is mentioned because we take what He so generously provided and twist it into manmade rules, squeezing the grace right out of it. Unhealthy and unhelpful fear brings about all different sorts of "fundamentalism," and it is important that we focus our efforts on our journey of recovery and desire to experience a deeper relationship with Jesus. Turning our eyes and attuning our hearts to God, we believe that going to meetings every day, calling our sponsor, and being involved in service work help us progress and heal.

It is also true that when we tithe, involve ourselves in ministry, do our best not to sin, and seek God with all our hearts, we also progress and heal. So, it is important that we follow the directions of our sponsor and spiritual advisors because they will help us find freedom from the dis-ease that has plagued us for so long.

We leave God to deal with the "thumpers" and focus our attention on the One who has all power and can relieve us of our addiction. Wherever God calls us and wherever we're placed, there will always be the temptation to think we must be perfect to serve Him well. But it is our faith in Jesus that God cares about.

Legalism, unbiblical expectations, and ungracious judgment have no place in our recovery and are contrary to God's will. As we walk with Jesus, our heads are held high and we gaze at the One who loves us, accepts us, and is the most supportive advocate we will ever know.

God, today help me accept the gift of Your forgiveness. Let me experience fellowship and companionship with You in new and exciting ways.

Day 27: *Our Hope Rests in God's Truth*

"And without faith it is impossible to please God, because anyone who comes to him must believe that he exists and that he rewards those who earnestly seek him." Hebrews 11:6

Christian Smith, a sociologist from the University of North Carolina, spent years studying the religious lives of teenagers. He concluded that most view God as a "combination divine butler and cosmic therapist." God exists to help them through their problems and achieve what they desire. Smith said that those holding this view of God are "primarily concerned with one's own happiness." With location 890 of 2958

The God most of us know is the one of convenience — the one we can yell and scream at or timidly pray to during the trauma and drama of life. Yet, once the yelling, screaming, and praying are over and the crisis resolves, we resume our lives either unwilling or not realizing that there are things we need to change.

Recovery calls our attention to the adolescent nature of our relationship with God. Most of us started using drugs, alcohol, food, or pornography when we were still children and it is at this point that our physical, mental, and spiritual development is arrested.

We are like unbridled horses and still feel the compulsion to go where we will and do what we want with an unrestrained nature beating wildly within us. It isn't until our lives were turned upside and we ran into the hot-wired fence that we finally stopped what we were doing and asked God for help.

The passion and lust for more didn't immediately leave us; yet we felt different and began to want more of God and less of ourselves. God took our brokenness and began to stir up in our hearts the desire for change. Recovery is too much for us to handle alone, and more and more we find that when we keep our eyes on God, we are more balanced even when things go wrong.

We are beginning to discover that God is alive within and around us as we go to meetings, work with a sponsor, and help others who suffer from addiction. Our hope rests in God's truth and not in who we are or who we aren't!

As we work Step Four and write about the wreckage, chaos, and pain of our past, we are humbled that God has already brought healing to our lives—healing because He is who He is and not because we did anything right or anything wrong! All God asks is that we walk toward Him in faith with the desire to know Him more.

God, today let me experience faith in You and, while I do need your comfort and healing, I want even more to walk with You in the garden of this life. Open me up to experience more of You – to know You and love You.

Day 28: *Unforsaken Seekers*

"The Lord is a refuge for the oppressed, a stronghold in times of trouble. Those who know your name trust in you, for you, Lord, have never forsaken those who seek you." Psalm 9:9–10.

It is comforting to know that God is a safe place for us when we feel pain, uncertainty, regret, and disappointment. His beautiful promise to never leave or reject us is one that we can trust. It is truly amazing that God, who named each star and numbered every single hair on our heads, promises to never abandon us like so many others have.

This is hard for us to imagine or believe because we have experienced such devastation and trouble in life. As we work Step Four, we begin to realize that it wasn't God who left us — we left Him!

It is in this life-changing step that we find out who we are and who we are not — and who God is and who He is not. He continues to show us that we are not our behaviors, nor are we the things we have done, no matter how heinous. Even though we are guilty of hurting other people, turning our backs on God, and being filled with self-righteous indignation, the same God who has numbered every hair on our head and named every star has proclaimed that we are innocent!

God continues to rescue us from ourselves and is our most committed champion and defender. He has won the war for our souls and will continue to defend us against all the accusations the evil one can hurl at us. The evil one's fiery arrows of accusation are poisonous, but our faith in Jesus is the antidote as we claim the victory of the cross.

Step Three has taught us about surrendering ourselves to a God who cares and Step Four provides us with the ability to acknowledge the burdens of our past and learn to forgive. Today, when trouble comes, we find our safe place in the love of God who will meet all our needs and find ourselves actually believing that He never will abandon us!

God, as I look upon my actions, sins, thoughts, and fears, help me trust You more. For God, you are the King of all, the creator of the heavens and the earth. Nothing is impossible for You.

Day 29: *Victims in Perpetuity*

"Make every effort to live in peace with everyone and to be holy; without holiness no one will see the Lord. See to it that no one falls short of the grace of God and that no bitter root grows up to cause trouble and defile many." Hebrews 12:14–15

It doesn't take long into the work of Step Four that we realize the bitter root of resentment is at the core of our pain and impacts how we experience life and relate to others. We are strong-willed, but addiction kicks it up into a riotous frenzy! The unmanageability of addiction has driven us to our knees, yet it isn't enough to rid us of unrealistic expectations, self-centered restlessness, boiling anger, and the belief that we are the perpetual victim.

However, recovery is about learning how to live as winners and overcomers. Many of us were victimized as children by situations beyond our control. Working a thorough Step Four may require extra effort in order for us to move past our sense of helplessness and find freedom. God says to cast all of our cares, worries, hurts, and disappointments on Him because He loves us more than we can even imagine.

We desperately want to believe this and find it necessary to examine closely how our innocent victimization became part of our addictive process. We are not responsible for the abuse and must reach deep within and honestly examine how we may have used our pain to gain the sympathy of others or to justify our addiction.

As we write about our resentments, it's surprising how we discover that we have injured ourselves much more than those who hurt us as children. Finding freedom from our resentments and pent-up historical anger requires that we break free from the strongholds that chained us to our addiction. Romans Twelve:2 tell us that we must be transformed by the renewing of our mind, and Step Four allows us to see into the patterns of how our thoughts and past experiences stir up internal conflict and influence our decisions.

While terrible things may have happened to us as children, we can be assured that God knows our every hurt and invites us to cast every memory and anxiety on Him. He is our Healer, Savior, Counselor, and Friend. We can count on Him.

God, today I will cast my every memory of hurt on You. Sometimes my pride gets in the way of remembering that You are in control. Help me be at peace with everyone, God, and learn how to forgive the same way You have forgiven me.

✝

Day 30: *We are not Junk!*

"He will cover you with his feathers, and under his wings you will find refuge; his faithfulness will be your shield and rampart. You will not fear the terror of night, nor the arrow that flies by day."
Psalm 91:4–5.

Suggested Reading: *Twelve Steps and Twelve Traditions, pg. 53.*

It is said often enough around the tables of our Twelve Step meetings that we don't have relationships: We take hostages!

Step Four is showing us how our important relationships were derailed and that we are still burned inside with shattered pieces of un-actualized hopes and dreams. Resentment is the fuel that stokes the fires of irritability, discontent, fear, anger, and restlessness. Distorted thoughts, unrealistic expectations, and self-destructive behavior patterns are also uncovered as we write about our failed romantic relationships.

It is mind-blowing to realize that addiction is the great pestilence of our day and has rocked the very foundation of who God created us to be in relation to Him and then one another. Unhealthy relationships were the ground zero of our addiction and we found ourselves doing awful things to people even though we were trying to find meaning and happiness.

Through Step Four, we've discovered that we're not quite the victims we had originally thought! Being the victim is familiar — the feelings are predictable — and we know how to deal with it. Being the victim is a really hard thing to give up. And it is even harder to admit that in many situations, we were the perpetrator of anger, hostility, and pain.

There is no benefit for us to live in toxic shame or guilt. And if we have learned anything in recovery, it is that God is in control. He's all but jumping up and down and furiously waving his arms shouting, "Hey, look at Me! You're created in My image — and I don't make junk!"

His love for us as deeply kids helps us stop looking around every corner in fear, worried that people are going to hurt us. We're realizing that even if they do, God will be there to help us through whatever pain may come. Man, we have been set free! God has shown us that He will never leave or forget us even in the darkest of times. Relieved, we're now ready to share this with someone else.

God, thank You for the freedom I have found in Step Four. I ask that you continue to light the way as I move forward into a new and trusting relationship with those You bring into my life.

✠

Acknowledgements:

A special thanks to:

My treatment counselor, Cindy C. I thank God every day that He uses perfectly broken people to heal;

To my sponsor, Jackie S. for getting down on bended knee with me in surrender;

To my sponsor, Lynn Mc who has loved me with a mother's heart and always kept my eyes focused on Jesus while holding my hand through times of grief and despair;

To Pastor's Jack Storry, Mark Molstre and Jim Ladd. Thank you for heeding the call to preach and for pointing me towards Jesus. The hope and inspiration you have given me through preaching God's Word are all throughout this devotional;

To my Mom and Dad, Bernie and Arlene, for praying for me and helping me with my daughter when I couldn't be the mom she needed;

To Pastor Don Matzat for helping me get this book published.

Bibliography:

Alcoholics Anonymous *Big Book,* (The Anonymous Press; 2008).

Alcoholics Anonymous, *Twelve Steps and Twelve Traditions,* (AA World Services; 2002).

Manning, Brennan, *Ragamuffin Gospel,* (Multnomah, 2005).

Matzat, Don,, *Christ-Esteem: Where the Search for Self-Esteem Ends,* (Harvest House, 1990).

Peterson, Eugene H,, *The Message,* (NavPress, 2016).

Stanley, Charles, *Landmines in the Path of the Believer: Avoiding the Hidden Dangers,* (Thomas Nelson, 2008).

Stanley Charles,, *When the Enemy Strikes: The Keys to Winning Your Spiritual Battles,* (Thomas Nelson, 2012).

Stanley Charles,, *Prayer, the Ultimate Conversation,* (Howard Books; 2013).

57385753R00158

Made in the USA
Middletown, DE
31 July 2019